Presented To:

Bingham Methodist
Church.

From:

Fiona Linday

Trusting that this book
will help you reach out to
the people on the Market.

Date:

12/12/23

Blessings!

The Father's Heart

The Father's Love

CHIDI OSUJI

Published By Open Scroll Publications

Copyright © 2023 Chidi Osuji
First Edition by:
Open Scroll Publications Ltd,
Kemp House, 160 City Road,
London, EC1V 2NX.
www.openscroll.co.uk

ISBN:978-1-9999856-9-1

A CIP catalogue record for this book is available from the British library.

Edited by Fiona Linday

Cover design and Typeset by Open Scroll Publications Ltd.

Printed in Great Britain.

Dedication

This book is dedicated to my grandchildren, Ella, Amarachi, Gabriel and Brielle, for being of good behaviour and popping your faces up during Grandma's Zoom meetings. You will carry on from where Grandma stops.

CONTENTS

Those who are wise will shine as bright as the sky, and those who lead many to righteousness will shine like the stars forever.
Daniel 12:3 NLT

Acknowledgements

I would like to appreciate my heavenly Father, 'Abba', who chose me and placed me where I am today. The author and finisher of my faith, without whom I could do nothing. Thank you, Lord! I love you, Lord!

I am truly indebted to my family, especially my grandchildren, Ella, Amarachi, Gabriel and Brielle, for your understanding and unshakable love, even when I missed some of your birthdays and school events because I was on the mission field or was preparing to go on mission. Also, my children, Uzoma, Ugo and Emeka and my daughters in-law Cynthia and Bianca, for allowing me to be unhospitable when I have left you at home to go to Bescot Market to minister after you have travelled hundreds of miles to visit me. May the Lord bless you immensely. Remember that you are a partaker of the blessings too.

I want to appreciate my beloved husband Dr Eze Charles Osuji, who is now in glory. I will always remember your words of encouragement and support for the calling on my life. Even on your sick bed, you reminded me to go to Bescot Market for the work of God. I know you have already received your 'Well done good and faithful servant' reward. Thank you, and God bless you.

I give heartfelt appreciation to my local Church, 'The Church at Junction 10', for creating the opportunity to run with the Missional Community model of leadership which came at a time that I was pregnant with a calling I didn't even know about. Also, the current elders, Rachel Jenkins, Kevin Davis and Joe Clark deserve my special thanks for their steady financial support, guidance and prayers for the ministry.

Thanks to the J10 admin staff: Vicky Foster, Philip Walker, Robert Read and the Youth pastor, Susan Gill for helping to resource 'Father's Heart' Missional Community through ordering or provision of materials. Your contributions are invaluable. Thank you for sending us out and supporting us. God bless you all abundantly.

To the 'Father's Heart' team, past and present, I salute you all. We have laboured together in the Lord's 'vine yard' through thick and thin. In all seasons of life, you have been there. We have dined together, laughed together and cried together when life has been difficult. We have been on this mission together and you are like the extension of my family. May you continue to shine as the brightness of the firmament and turn many to righteousness as the stars forever. Your crown of glory awaits you.

The Father's Heart ministry project team, Charis Bible College class of 2020, Milli Williams, Osaze Imarhiagbe, Derek Silk, Maureen Freeman and Innocentia Ezea, I thank you for being on this journey with me knowing full well that it was a church ministry. You worked tirelessly on this project and gave your all, not because you wanted to pass your exams but because of the passion you had and continue to have for this ministry. The vision was made plain and you ran with it. Thank you for heeding the prompt of the Holy Spirit to join me.

To Lucy Curtis-Prior, it has been an absolute pleasure working with you all through this project. Your proof-reading skills are at a different level and your passion for it is clearly obvious. I have always appreciated you as my college tutor then, but more so now that you have devoted your time to proof-read my book at no cost. Respect!! May your pen not run dry in Jesus' name.

Thank you, Fiona Linday, for taking me on this coaching journey to edit my book. Your professionalism is truly to be admired and the joy that you bring each time is worthy of praise. I have learnt so much from you, and this is to a great partnership for future books to come. Thank you for the personal sacrifices you have made to accommodate this project. It is greatly appreciated.

Many thanks to my nephew, Ikechi Marizu Atuonwu, for your contributions of art concepts. May your God given talents make you relevant and more visible to the world. Blessings!

Last but most certainly not the least, my gratitude goes to Pastor Michael Ekwulugo of Open Scroll Publications for your words of encouragement and excellent work with this project. God bless you!

But if I say I'll never mention the LORD or speak in his name, his word burns in my heart like a fire.It's like a fire in my bones!I am worn out trying to hold it in!I can't do it!

Jeremiah 20:9 NLT

The Father's Heart, The Father's Love
Synopsis

I stuttered as a child, with little or no confidence at all in public speaking, until the Lord healed me at the age of thirty. And now, I find myself with a burden to fulfil the call of God on my life, which requires me to use my healed tongue as a celebration of God's faithfulness. This burden was like fire in my bones that I could not lay down. When the opportunity came, I knew I could not hold back, and despite the challenges in starting, I was determined to do it afraid.

The waiting and excitement created a suspense that I could not describe, but it did come, and it is a fulfilment of all that I had expected and much more. 'The Father's Heart, The Father's Love' takes you through the journey of starting a ministry or business. The favour, kindness from strangers, testimonies of lives changed and transformed, are obvious evidences for all to see that truly HE who has promised is faithful to accomplish HIS purposes. The Scripture says that 'a great and effective door has been opened unto you but there are many adversaries.' We were given a mandate to love, befriend, and invest the Kingdom of God into people's lives. We were not trained and had no clue about evangelism, but we were willing, ready, and available and the Holy Spirit took over. HE was our teacher, and HE remains in charge.

This is Father's business. We are co-labourers in HIS vineyard. The seeds we sow today, another will water, and another will harvest but only God gives the increase.

We have grown and waxed stronger because we know that HE is with us always and will confirm HIS words through the signs and wonders that have followed and will continue to follow. It is a very difficult thing to love the unlovable but that is what Jesus did and that is what HE has commissioned us to do.

As Christians, we have failed in many ways to reach the least and the lost. This has resulted in many people turning away from the church while others who were in church have left and vowed not to return because they were wounded in the house of God by the very people who should have cared for them. Jesus did not call us to build gigantic buildings and warm the pews, much as the church as a structural building is important. HE asked us to 'Go and make disciples of all men, baptizing them in the name of the Father and of the Son and of the Holy Spirit.'

Focus is an essential element in any ministry or business and should be taken seriously. Our walk with God will help us maintain that focus and therefore determine whether we grow or fail in that venture. This principle has been pivotal during our journey. Intimacy with the Father helps to navigate the course of our ministry, because without divine guidance and direction, challenges like the lockdown as a result of the COVID-19 pandemic could paralyse or end any venture. In this instance however, our venture grew to a new level.

The author has shared her experience of starting a ministry and running with it. This way of doing things is not just applicable to ministries, but to businesses and other ventures also. Mistakes were made. However, that is the way to learn also. When we stop what we're doing, take stock, and identify the shortfalls, we can course correct and launch out again. When we apply this method of working, the level of growth achieved will be significant.

In conclusion, whatever is on your heart, step out in faith and run with it. Do not wait until you have ticked all the boxes, otherwise you will never start. Do not let the passion for that calling fade away and do not underestimate what you are able to achieve with the leading of the Holy Spirit. Try not to compare yourself with people who have stepped out and failed. Rather, learn from those who have excelled in their ministries or businesses, and be encouraged. Remember, 'HE who has called you is faithful and will accomplish that which HE has started in you'.

Therefore do not cast away your confidence, which has great reward. For you have need of endurance, so that after you have done the will of God, you may receive the promise:

"For yet a little while, And He[a] who is coming will come and will not [b]tarry.

Now the[c] just shall live by faith; But if anyone draws back, My soul has no pleasure in him."
Hebrews 10:35-38 NKJV

Endorsements

Chidi has obediently and sacrificially followed the calling and vision Jesus gave her, soaking it in prayer and founding it on the Word of God. She has heard God's whisper and stepped out of her comfort zone, following the strategy God gave her for reaching and discipling, delivering and blessing the people she and her team meet at Bescot Market. She has adapted, planned, prayed, fasted, course corrected and followed the voice of God. She has persevered, learnt from others, laboured away with passion, positivity, compassion and a servant heart. The testimonies recounted in this book are nothing short of remarkable, and are a clear demonstration of God at work in 21st century Britain. I am truly humbled to have walked alongside Chidi and cheered her on as she walks the walk of faith, mission and discipleship in her life. I recommend this book as an example of what can happen when an ordinary woman is inspired to follow an extraordinary God.

Mrs. Mary Banks

Missional Communities Leader, The Church at Junction 10

In her own words, 'Bescot Market is a place of joy, laughter, friendship...and pain,' which is a perfect summary of a ministry founded by a faithful, unassuming woman. But don't let that description fool you. 'The Father's Heart, The Fathers Love', journeys how everyday people can share powerfully the love of Jesus with everyday people. Through the pain of obstacles, practical and personal, Sister Chidi and her faithful team, have literally gone into the market place, sharing the joy of Jesus, befriending traders, and customers in the process. This book, this personal testimony, should inspire anyone trying to do the work of the Evangelist, even if they wouldn't describe themselves as such.

Elder Kevin Davis, The Church at Junction 10

If you are feeling led to venture forwards into the thing that the Lord has called you for, reading this book will certainly stir you to get your thinking cap on and start planning without delay. At the same time, by her example, Chidi will remind us of the absolute necessity of hearing from the Lord at every stage, and only then responding in obedience to his instructions.

You will be touched by the many stories in these pages of individuals from all walks of life, faiths, and backgrounds, who through Chidi and her team encountered the Living God, receiving salvation, peace, freedom and answered prayer - and the testimonies keep coming! You will be impressed with the way in which Chidi has so carefully stewarded the task and responsibility of running 'Father's Heart Ministry' - a unique community outreach project to her busy local market. This account of her journey reveals how much of an adventure it has been, with joys and delights as well as situations to overcome. Read the book and be inspired and strengthened to step out and do likewise.

Lucy Curtis-Prior, Friend and Cheerer-on-er

This book is a practical outline of the calling, preparation and launching out into the dynamic field of evangelism, which makes the whole process easy.

I have been particularly inspired by the live account of the contents of this wonderful book when I gave the author an opportunity to share her practical experience to a large Christian audience. The many miracles and testimonies demonstrate how God supports his work and calling. There is a silent cry for God in many souls awaiting to be reached. I highly recommend it. The Bescot Market evangelism model is a God ordained phenomenon that can be replicated in many cities through partnership working.

Rabbi (Dr) Sam Ejide, Co-Founder Kabod Glory Revival

CHAPTER ONE

IN THE BEGINNING

My Call To Evangelise

My paternal grandmother would call out "'Atujuo!' Let us go. We are going to be late if we do not hurry up!" Atujuo" is short for Atujuobi, meaning comforter or pacifier. She called me that because my father was an only child, although he had four half-brothers because in those days women arranged for their husbands to marry another wife if they could not have children themselves. My grandmother, fondly called Daa, had only my dad and, like Sarah in the Bible, she had arranged for another wife for her husband, my grandfather, and she had more children for him.

Carrying on with my story, where was Daa taking me at about 5:30am, you may ask? We were going to church for morning prayer. With her Tilley lamp, we would wade through the Cocoyam leaves, wet with the morning dew, to get to her church. Daa was a deaconess in the Christ Apostolic Church and followed her Christian faith passionately. Her attendance to church for morning prayers was a daily routine which she did religiously and was still available for other church events all through the week. This experience with my grandmother was possible because of the Biafra civil war that broke out in Nigeria from 1967 to

1969, when my parents took us back home to Ntalakwu Oboro in Abia State, Nigeria. My parents were also devout Christians and they too followed and served God in the Methodist Church till they went to be with the Lord. That was the background I came from.

I have always been involved in one ministry or another. Growing up in a family that made Christ the core of their lives, I knew I would also be in one form of service or another. As I mentioned in my first book, 'The Victorious Journey,' I started singing in the church choir at the age of nine years and I have not looked back since.

This is not because of family, although that plays a part, but because of the calling on my life - our upbringing and environment positions us for life. There is an old proverb that states that an apple does not fall far from the tree. Although it is debatable in general terms that children follow after their parents to serve in ministry, it still applies.

I recall my parents arriving early to church most Sundays, either to get the church ready or for rehearsal before the commencement of services, midweek services, women's fellowship meetings, men's fellowship meetings and choir practices on different days of the week, lay-preaching, and the list goes on.

A good relationship between parents and children in ministry is very essential and should be encouraged. When the Lord has done something for us or when our lives have been impacted in any way by the teachings of the life of Christ, we want to let people around us know about it because they are the future. We should encourage and teach our children to be bearers of good news. We should not stop telling the stories of God's faithfulness to our children because the Children of Israel were rebuked for not telling their children of the great deliverance God wrought for them when HE delivered them from the hand of Pharoah and parted the Red Sea for them to cross over on the dry ground. The Old Testament is full of instances where references were made to fathers and their children or mothers and their children but, in this book, we will be mentioning more about the relationship between fathers and their children, whether it be good or bad.

I had a wonderful relationship with my father, fondly called Dede. I was the only girl of my parents and the first of five children, and much as my dad made me feel so special, it was also the same for my brothers. Dede made us feel so special and he had enough love to go round, even to other people around him. My father was a perfect example of commitment. He started taking me to choir practice from an early age and when I was nine years old, I was singing in the adult choir in our church.

And I have not looked back because of this foundation already laid, not just by my earthly parents but more importantly by my heavenly Father. I continued attending choir practices with my dad until I went to secondary school where I lived in a boarding house. I was raised a Methodist and went to a Methodist girls' secondary school in Ovim, Abia State in Nigeria. Part of the life and character of Methodism is the prevalence of hymns, so when I started school, I continued with my school choir and I have always sung all my life. Unlike my dad however, I am still not able to play a musical instrument yet. This is because I have not followed it through, but hopefully that will change soon. Thankfully, my own children play the drums and piano.

When I left secondary school and went on to further my education, I carried on singing, and worship brings me very close to God. As I worshiped, I found out that I had a passion and burden to pray and intercede for people around me, and into situations. As Christians, we are called to pray because, as we know, a prayerless Christian is a powerless Christian. The scripture tells us in Luke 18:1b that men always ought to pray and not faint, and in other portions of scripture we are encouraged to pray without ceasing. Samuel considered it a sin for him not to pray for the Children of Israel. In First Samuel 12:23 Samuel said, "Moreover as for me, God forbid that I should sin against the Lord in ceasing to pray for you: but I will teach you the good and the right way."

During my times of prayer, God has opened my eyes to see visions. I also have had prophecies spoken over me which were in line with what God showed me in my dreams or had given me as a word during these times. One such dream I had mentioned previously in my first book but will share again because it is key to what this book is about, and it goes thus: I was in a dream, chatting with a group of people on the street, and a man walked up to me and said, "Do it as they did in Acts 10:30-47." When I woke up, I read this portion of scripture intently and it became clear what God was calling me into, but I didn't have any experience of evangelism apart from the dance and drama I was involved with years ago in

Bangor, North Wales before we moved to Walsall in 1996 and my involvement as part of the worship team with the Full Gospel Business Men's Fellowship. This happened years ago between 1992 and 1994 where we ministered at events, breakfast meetings or during our usual weekly meetings. For someone who used to stammer badly but was healed by God, I was still a bit of an introvert. My thoughts were, "How on earth am I going to do this?" but I knew it had nothing to do with me and I was determined to do what I believed God was calling me to do. I had no confidence sharing my faith but, like Paul, I considered it a privilege to be called in this way.

At that moment, I put all my dependency on God, knowing that where I fell short as a person, God's strength would be made manifest, and He would carry me through. God saw something in me that I did not see in myself, just like my earthly father who said to me "You will be a good nurse," but I did not see it myself at the time. I am very grateful to God who enabled me to put the limitations of my flesh aside and put my trust in HIM. In First Timothy 1:12 it says:"And I thank Christ Jesus our Lord, who hath enabled me, for HE counted me faithful, putting me into the ministry".

My thoughts were: how on earth am I going to do this? But I knew it had nothing to do with me and I was determined to do what I believed God was calling me to do.

CHAPTER TWO

STEPPING OUT ONTO THE MISSION FIELD

In my church, an opportunity came up at a time that I had decided to wait for direction from the Lord. I knew HE was leading me to do something, but I truly was not sure what it was about. My beloved husband and I had just stepped down from the leadership of the international group in our church after nine years because we felt the time had come for us to do so.

I joined the intercessory group led by Barbara Rowley and my husband Charles joined the Saturday morning prayer group. I felt so at home in this group and had the space to wait on the Lord for direction. During this period, there were lot of dreams and revelations, prophecies, and words from the Lord from different people which I didn't quite understand then but needed the space to pray and seek God about for clear direction, and I had space to do so. Under the leadership of Barbara, we really prayed, prayer walked the area, and her husband would let us into the board room where he worked and we would pray for the area and intercede for the community, the local authorities and government at large.

God did some amazing things in the area. We saw a change

in the things we prayed about for example, there used to be some notorious high-rise buildings in that area that were a breeding ground for drug dealing and abuse, prostitution, and muggings. The buildings were demolished and rebuilt, resulting in low crime and reduced antisocial behaviours.

There were also council officers that God miraculously realigned for things to begin to change. The area has been transformed ever since and there are lots of other testimonies I could mentioned but we will continue, as there are so many miraculous things that God did at that time and continues to do. It was a privilege to be part of this special group of people. As Barbara was considering laying down the leadership of this group, there was a meeting in church by Jonathan Bentley, the then Senior Pastor of my church, The Church at Junction Ten, Walsall. Popularly known as J10 Church, Walsall. I sat and listened intently as he talked about a new model to be introduced in church called the Missional Communities. He encouraged anyone with a passion or gifting to prayerfully consider getting involved. The Missional Communities were meant to nurture, support, and grow people in different aspects of ministry; to step out in faith with a small group or community with a shared vision based on exploring and working out a lifestyle of faith, investing in our relationship with God and each other and finally finding ways of loving our town and being part of its life.

There will be an element of 'UP' that is a time of gathering, an element of 'IN' a time of refreshing in the presence of God and being poured into, and another element of 'OUT' which is the point of reaching out to the community of people around us. There would be support from the church and we would never be alone in the mission field. When I heard all this, it warmed my heart, and I knew immediately that it was an opportunity to step out. Although we were asked to go home and pray about it, within me, I was convinced this was the moment. After that meeting, I went straight to tell the pastor that I was ready. My heart was one hundred percent ready, but I still did not know what I was doing or how to go about it, but the passion and desire to serve in this way totally consumed me.

God had been preparing my heart for this time and honestly, nothing else mattered. I would think about it, pray about it, and waited patiently on God for the next move.

I had a cancer scare at that time and my husband was very concerned about me, but I had so much peace. I was full of excitement and at the same time nervous, especially when my flesh crept in to remind me of how I used to stutter, but I knew that HE who had called me was faithful. If HE healed me for this purpose, then who am I to think or say otherwise? I was determined to do it afraid so long as I was living in HIS will. I could relate to Jeremiah, the prophet, when he said:

> *But his word was in mine heart as a burning fire shut up in*
> *my bones, and I was weary with forbearing,*
> *and I could not stay.*
> **Jeremiah 20:9 KJV**

When this was eventually announced to the wider 'church', members were invited to contact those who had already stepped out or indicated where their interest lay, depending on where they 'themselves' felt the Spirit of God was leading them. A good few people showed interest in my group and at this point, we had no name, but we all knew it was about sharing the gospel of Jesus Christ to the people out there who do not know HIM yet. We began to meet to pray and seek God about this and so much came out of this time. We would meet on the second and last Thursdays of the month and we started to receive words from the

Lord. I remember people saying to me "Draft a letter and invite some of your friends in church or people you know that are mature in the things of God." I did not follow that counsel for these reasons: I had already said to the group that we would continue to wait on the Lord until he instructed us 'step by step' on the details of how to go about things. If we did not hear, we would have carried on praying and waiting, but soon enough, God began to give words, dreams, and scriptures to different members of the team, and I will be mentioning some of what we received as we progress. It is very important in ministry that we hear God clearly on the things we are praying about and not what our flesh is dictating, or emulate how "Aunty Sue" or "Uncle Fred" did it. The flesh must die so that Christ can increase in us. It might be a good idea, but is it a God idea? This, for me, is very important in ministry, that we do not belong because we like the people in the group but rather because we are sent or called into that ministry.

CHAPTER THREE

WE HAVE A NAME

All that I have mentioned about the Missional Communities and this group started in 2011. When the different groups were formed, one of our church leaders called Mary Banks had the responsibility of coordinating all the groups. She worked so hard to support all the groups because it was a big step for most of us. We had passion and we knew we had heard from God, but we did not know how things were going to pan out. I certainly did not know how. It was an exciting time and Mary was there, right from the start. The groups were quite diverse, according to people's different giftings; some had a business model focus like a coffee shop, equipping and skilling up people for cooking and confectioneries, while others were ministry-focused. We all had one thing in common and that was mission.

Mary visited me with another mutual friend as I was recovering from an operation in April 2012. We were chatting away, having a good catch up, when she asked me a question; Have you thought about a name for your group?

My response was that I was praying about it and would let her know when I had. Towards the end of that visit, they prayed for me. While Mary was praying, the Holy Spirit dropped two words in my spirit "Father's Heart." This was kept in my heart and I pondered over it, and continued to pray that God would confirm this to me and within one week of me receiving those two words from the Holy Spirit, it was confirmed on two different occasions, and I knew straight away that it was the name God wanted me to call the group. I now contacted Mary Banks and Jonathan Bentley, the Senior Pastor of our church at the time, and told them the name.

As I thought about the name, I knew that it was the right name for this ministry. The scripture tells us in John 3:16, "For God so loved the world that HE gave HIS only begotten Son, that whosoever believes in HIM should not perish but have eternal life." God saw man's sinful nature and, out of love, sent Jesus to die for the atonement of the sins of mankind. Jesus came to show us the way and people need to hear that, because in our world today, the only time the name of Jesus comes out of some people's mouth, is when it comes as a swear word or blasphemy. How sad!!

The truth is that Jesus came that we might be reconciled to the Father. The sins we had committed were offences punishable by death (spiritual death). You might ask yourself, "What did I do wrong? I pay my taxes, I do good to other people and wish them well, so I will go to heaven when the time comes." No, it does not work like that. It is not about what we have done or what we have not done, but about what Jesus did on the cross of Calvary for us all. Sin is inherent in man because of the disobedience of Adam and Eve. Because of that, the nature of man is sinful, BUT the good news is that every sin we have ever committed or will ever commit has already been paid for when Jesus died on the cross.

Every man is seeking God and we want to hear HIM, but the ONLY way to God is through Jesus Christ. I liken it to someone who committed an offence punishable by death and has been sentenced as a result, and another completely innocent person comes and takes his punishment of death so that the offender could go free. That is what Jesus did for us all when HE died on the cross. HE said, "It is finished." HE paid it in full. We are free but we still need to confess Jesus Christ, believe with our hearts, and accept HIM into our lives by faith as LORD and Saviour, and then we will have eternal life. This is good news and good news must be shared.

Once we got the name, we continued in prayer for direction and clarity. I made it clear that nothing of the flesh was going to take the upper hand and we were determined for it to remain so, because it is not about us but about HIM who sent us. The team began to grow in number, with people of same passion and burden. Our vision at that moment was to seek God concerning our church, community, nation, and each other. Our guiding scriptures came during our time of prayer, from myself and another team member, and they are as follows: "Your people will rebuild the ancient ruins and will raise up the age-old foundations; you will be called Repairer of Broken Walls, Restorer of Streets with Dwellings." Isaiah 58:12, and the second one is from Second Chronicles 7:14 "If my people, who are called by my name, will humble themselves and pray and seek my face and turn from their wicked ways, then will I hear from heaven and will forgive their sins and will heal their land". These scriptures have guided us ever since.

Some of you will rebuild the deserted ruins of your cities. Then you will be known as a rebuilder of walls and a restorer of homes.
Isaiah 58:12 NLT

If my people, which are called by my name, shall humble themselves, and pray, and seek my face, and turn from their wicked ways; then will I hear from heaven, and will forgive their sin, and will heal their land.

2 Chronicles 7:14 KJV

CHAPTER FOUR

INTIMACY WITH GOD

When God calls us into anything new, hearing HIM clearly is very important. It must be said that no matter our previous experience in serving God, when it comes to a new ministry, we need to seek fresh direction from God, otherwise it becomes our flesh acting. It is not about how many ministries we have led in the past and how successful they were, important as that is, we need to know that every calling or new assignment comes with new direction and grace for that particular calling or office. So, spending time in prayer with the Holy Spirit is key and for the next six months, we met every second and fourth Thursdays of the month to seek God, pray, listen, and share what we had received with one another. It was during this time that God gave me a clear instruction for us to "Go and befriend them, love them, and invest the kingdom of God into their hearts if they were open", and that is what we have continued to do. In the team, we had up to sixteen people at one point made up of people from all walks of life. It was a time of great bonding, team building, but mostly a time to draw close to God. We had the space to fast and pray on a few occasions, something we needed to do more frequently as a group.

Initially, I was thinking it would be a street evangelism or outreach ministry because of the dream that I had which I mentioned earlier, but as time went on, a word came from one of us that we should consider going into a nearby market to scope the area.

We noted that and began to pray and enquire about a nearby market called Bescot Market. We needed to know who ran it and how they operated. Also, were we required to do anything? We thought about the demographics, culture, and social orientation of the market. It is a marketplace, and we would expect to see all sorts of people of all ages, race, colour, and all other variables.

We began thinking of how to engage with people and respect everyone, whether they were trading or buying. Jesus died for us all. Every person we see whether they go to church or not, Jesus laid down His life for them and they need to hear that. We were all assigned tasks to enquire about different things. One of the core members of the team, Juliet Chikore, knew someone who worked with the council. She contacted her for advice as to how we could go about establishing ourselves in the market, and she came back with the information we needed. We had books donated to us from church members and we ended up with so much materials, including post cards and leaflets or tracts. Judith Oliver was good with crafts and she made some practical things for children to play with if they had time. We got other things like a display board, banner and so on.

As we prepared the practical things, we also prepared spiritually. None of us had any formal training to evangelise but we were willing, available, teachable and we were ready. When God calls, HE doesn't call the qualified, but HE qualifies the called. God looks at the heart and equips us with the grace and faith required for that calling and that is why, liking a ministry or being friends with people in a ministry is not enough reason to join that ministry. It must be Holy Spirit led. We were not eloquent or extroverts, but God laid a burden in our hearts for the lost and we stepped out in faith. I have to say that there are no exclusions in this group. It is open to 'whoever' has that hunger in them to tell people about Jesus and see them come into the family of God. Such people are very welcome.

The Holy Spirit gave me a dream, and in that dream, people were just flocking into my house where we met for Bible study.

There was also another occasion when I was fasting, not particularly for Father's Heart though, and the Holy Spirit dropped a scripture into my heart, Jeremiah 32:27, and it states, "Behold, I am the LORD, the God of all flesh: is there anything too hard for me?" I received it with thanks as I was believing God for many things at this time. I prayed about it as I drove home from my Nursing job that day.

When I got in, I went straight to my bedroom and began to pray. Reflecting on that scripture and my day, the Lord gave me a picture of a bird with one of its wings broken. There were feathers everywhere and you could tell the bird had been in some type of contest and was badly wounded. As I stared at it for a long time, it seems I lifted up my eyes and saw the bird flying in the sky and immediately I remembered the song, "Divine Exchange", "restoring what was broken, so we may fly again." I praised and thanked God that whatever the problem was, it had been sorted out by God HIMSELF.

This is what I believe that God is sending us out to do: to be "Repairers of the Breach" and repairers of broken wings so that people can fly again. When we begin to share the word of God, broken lives, broken health, emotions, finances, are repaired through the knowledge and application of the word of God. During one of the meetings, another member of the team brought a word from the Lord, and it stated that "although things were slow sometimes, we were to persevere and trust HIM and not to give up and even if it is one or two people that we engaged with, we were to continue because HE is with us to perform HIS word." That was an encouraging word from Abigail Obia. As a group, we pondered and prayed about it. We have always known that God was with us.

Another instance was, I was worrying about something when the Lord reminded me that it was HIS business, not mine. We are co-labourers with Christ and should not shoulder any burden at all. If HE sends us on any mission, then HE is more than able to meet the need that could arise there. This has been a great source of strength to me all these years. Remember, our flesh must die and give way and even when we think that things are not going the right way, HE knows everything. HE will fix it. First Corinthians 3:9 says, "For we are God's fellow workers; we are God's field; we are God's building".

God is the senior partner in every work we do for HIM. When we do it God's way and we face challenges, then HE will also deal with the challenges so that we do not have to be burdened in that work. We might be the Jesus that many people will see today, but we will never be the Saviour. Jesus is the only Saviour and HE is more than able.

Preparation time is not wasted time and should be taken seriously, no matter how eager we are to step out or launch out, it is important to wait for the green light before stepping out. Waiting gives us speed and access. When we wait, we avoid hard knocks and setbacks. The direction is always precise and on point. So, let us wait for the green light.

In Acts 10:1-47, the scripture tells us how an angel had appeared to Cornelius while he was fasting and praying to God. The angel of the Lord told him that his prayers were answered. The angel gave Cornelius instructions to send men to Joppa and invite Peter to his house. At the same time an angel also appeared to Peter, who was also praying, and asked him not to call unclean what God created and not refuse to eat it. He did not quite understand this at this point, but while he thought about it the men that Cornelius had sent appeared at the place where he was lodging enquiring after him. As he pondered, the Holy Spirit said to Peter that God had sent the men and he was to go with them. Peter went to Cornelius's house with the men and on reaching there, he found that Cornelius had invited his household to come and listen to what Peter had to say.

In those days, the Jews and the Gentiles would not normally be seen doing anything together but because God had already appeared to both men and given them instructions, their meeting was very cordial and there was no confusion. They explained their encounters to each other and Peter went on to preach the gospel to them all and while he preached, the Holy Spirit came upon them and they spoke in other tongues and magnified the Lord. They were also water baptised afterwards. God is truly no respecter of persons, HE loves us all and it does not matter our race, age, colour, educational background, or bank balance. Jesus loves us all enough to lay down HIS life for each one of us.

By this time, we had contacted the Market Manager Steve Evans, and had a good chat with him. A date was set for our initial visit which turned out to be very warm and friendly, and I knew immediately that it was going to be a good partnership. He was our person of peace to fulfil God's mission in the market.

CHAPTER FIVE

LAUNCHING OUT

We went straight to the Market Manager's office and I introduced the team. He also introduced the market team to us. This was to be the beginning of a very wonderful partnership. He told us straight away that other stall holders would pay for their stalls because that is how the council generates revenue from the market, but we would not be required to pay because we were classed as a charity. However, we would be assigned our stall after the main traders had got their special spots, which meant that we would not have a designated spot. This was fine by us because it gave us the opportunity to make new friends with the traders each time and get to know them. We also saw God's hand in it, because although it might seem that we were not a priority, we always ended up with the best spot that most suited our purpose for being there.

This was very difficult initially, because some of the shoppers, hoping to see us on the same spot each time, found they had to search a little bit more to find us. Some of the traders did not want to see us at all and they did not hide it either. One of the words the Lord gave us was from First Corinthians 16:9, and it states, "For a great and effective door has been opened unto me, and there are many adversaries." We were already aware of these oppositions and frosty neighbours because the Lord had told us this in the place of prayer. This was not obvious initially because we started with prayer walking the market for a few times and getting to know the people first. Our routine was to have breakfast together, pray, and then go to the market. We would all come back after each visit to give feedback and share our experiences. This was to help us with planning and knowing what to expect in the future. Some of the feedbacks from the initial visits were as follows: some people were overwhelmed but not frightened, some had a sense of peace, friendships were forged, prayer requests were received, and the favour of God was notably huge. For me, I saw the Bescot location as God having a great sense of humour.

My beloved husband was also a member of the group. He knew that Bescot Market was not my favourite place to visit at all because prior to all this, he would want to stop at the market on our way back from church sometimes, to buy one thing or another, because he could get some hard-to-find items there at a reduced price. Each time he would pull up there, my mood would change and the next question would be, "Are you coming out?" My response would always be "NO." I would stay in the car and refuse to come out. He would even buy me some meat to entice me but it did not work. I did not like Sunday markets at all, but I would gladly go to the shops on a Sunday, fill my trolley with all sorts, and not feel any guilt. How ridiculous was that? Anyway, when Bescot Market came up during our prayer time, my heart sank within me. Nobody knew about my dislike for Sunday markets except my family and I did not tell anyone else about it. I was determined to go to wherever God sent us regardless of how I felt. I remember that a few days before we went to the market, I drove to the market car park, sat in my car, and began to pray, hoping that God would confirm that Bescot Market was not the location he was calling us to. As I sat and prayed, I felt nothing but peace. It was then I knew that it was of the Lord and my response to Him was, "Where you lead Lord, I will follow, so let your will be done." I was surprised how peaceful it was for me, even though I did not know what I was doing. Another strange thing for me was that no matter how tired I felt before going to the market, the moment I got there, I felt a surge of strength and a spring in my step, and I still feel the same today. Others in the team have also testified of the same experience.

Other feedback we had was about the things we had identified as needs going forward. These were things like plastic table covers, different coloured light bulbs to attract people, balloons, lollies, and cupcakes were to be used as draws, paper weights, a banner and badges to identify us. We thought it would be good to run two sessions each visit so that we could cover long periods of time with a view to having a changeover of volunteers at some point. We started putting these things into place and people were prepared to sow into the kingdom by using their own money to purchase the required items.

We did not have to ask the church for anything except on a few occasions. There was a buzz in the team and a bond was developing that I could not have imagined. Whenever it was Bescot week, we always added the weather into our prayer request and God favoured us tremendously. Although there were times when the weather was contrary, we were all determined not to let that stop us. I recall stopping at one of the traders' stalls as we prayer walked to share the love of Christ and he began to tease us, asking us to stop the rain, and then he would believe. We prayed for the rain to cease, not to prove a point but because we also needed dry weather. Shortly after we prayed, we continued with the prayer walk and a few minutes later, we all realised the rain had stopped, and this gentleman acknowledged it. He waved as we walked past and we all smiled and gave God all the glory and that was the case throughout our stay in the market that day, it did not rain. About six years later, we met him again as we prayer walked the market, and he remembered us and talked about what God had done on that day. He also asked us to wait, saying that he had something for us, which he had brought us, and he had been carrying it around all these years, hoping to see us one day. After what seemed like a good ten minutes of waiting, he brought out a crucifix he had bought and insisted we should have it. Although we did not need it, out of courtesy, we accepted his thank you gift that day, but soon gave it to another person in the market who needed it. That was his way of appreciating what God had done in the market that day, and it gave us the opportunity to have a good conversation with him and encouraged him in the Lord.

Our vision at this point was to take the gospel of Jesus Christ to the least, the lost and the marginalised. As I mentioned earlier, none of us in the team had any formal training or coaching in evangelism but because we were willing, available, and teachable, we learnt a lot from the time we spent praying. The Holy Spirit, our helper, our teacher and our standby, was always with us.

CHAPTER SIX

GO AND LOVE THEM

The world we live in today is in dire need of the truth. In John 14:6, Jesus said to Thomas, one of His disciples,

> *I am the way, the truth, and the life: no one comes to the Father except through me.*
> **John 14:6**

If Jesus is the way, we must have HIM in our lives to know where we ought to go. Without HIM, we walk in darkness. Knowing the Truth and having the Truth is what will help us to navigate life so that we do not grope in darkness. God loves us and wants us to come to a saving knowledge of HIM. The knowledge of God and an understanding of how much HE loves us is very liberating, but until we know that, we will still be existing instead of living. God sent Jesus to mankind that we may have life, and have life to the full (John 10:10). Living life without the knowledge of God's redeeming love means that we are existing and not necessarily living life to the full.

> *My people perish due to lack of knowledge*
> **Hosea 4:6**

People are searching and asking questions about existence and life after the here and now. If we are not out there to make them aware of how much Jesus loves them and what HE did for us all on the cross of Calvary, they will fall into the wrong hands. We have let God down in many ways because we have failed to tell people of God's love for them and equip them with the word of God. That is why the devil has reached some people and equipped them with lies, extremism, guns, drugs, violence, and the list go on.

In John 3:16, It says, "For God so loved the world that HE gave HIS only begotten son that whosoever believes in HIM should not perish but have everlasting life," and in John 15:13, Jesus said to his disciples, "Greater love has no one than this, than to lay down one's life for his friends."

Notice that Jesus calls us friends. HE laid down HIS life willingly and HE died for sins HE did not commit. HE took our place and died our death, that we should no longer be subject to the yoke of slavery of sin. Past sins, present and future sins, have all been paid for in full. This is good news, and everyone needs to hear this. It is for this reason that God sent us to tell everyone that whosoever believes in HIM should not perish but have everlasting life. The instruction God gave us was to go and love them, befriend them, and invest into them the kingdom. In the letter of Paul to the Romans, in Romans 10:11-15 says, "For the Scripture says, "whoever believes on HIM will not be put to shame." For there is no distinction between Jew and Greek, for the same Lord over all is rich to all who call upon HIM. For "whoever calls on the name of the Lord shall be saved." How then shall they call on Him in whom they have not believed? And how shall they hear without a preacher? And how shall they preach unless they are sent?" This is why we do what we do. Everyone deserves to know that Jesus died for their sins and only HE can save them. There are many followers of Jesus all over the earth but only ONE Saviour, Jesus Christ. The love of Christ is for "whoever believes" but they need to know that, and to be able to decide for themselves.

It must be said that sharing the good news of Jesus Christ is not by force or by threatening people. It is about sharing the truth of the gospel which can set people free from the bondage of sin. There are many types of evangelism, and we must be careful that we do not Bible bash or threaten people with Hell fire. The instruction is clear: love them and befriend them, and we have seen tremendous results in the marketplace. Just a smile or simple "hello," will draw someone to you. The method we use is relational evangelism.

Genuinely asking after people and getting to know them always works. If they are happy and ready to learn more, then we can tell them more and give them leaflets or tracts, books, CDs and DVDs. Initially, it was difficult for us because we wanted to engage with them but it's a marketplace, and people come to either window shop or to buy. So, engaging with the people was difficult. We considered the option of getting them to complete a survey, just to find out what they wanted, but that did not work because of time and, needless to say that some of the things we had factored in at the beginning were not put to good use or implemented. We continued to review our strategies and plan depending on the feedback we were getting after each visit. Course correction is key. You do not impose anything on anybody, but you learn the culture and social inclinations of the people and adapt accordingly. We have given out drinks on very warm summer days or tea and coffee on cold days. We are there to love them and get to know them.

People open up to you when they know you. We have seen hundreds of seeds sown through sharing the word, giving out free materials to both old and young, giving out cakes on Father's Day, as well as balloons and lollies. The seeds we sow today can be nurtured or watered by someone else and harvested by yet another.

The harvest comes from God and all the fruits are for HIS kingdom. The size of the harvest depends on what stage people are at. For some people, with a little testimony and sharing the love of God, they accept Christ. For others, you might need to invest a little more time. Some of these people are regulars at the market and they have come to know us and would stop for a chat.

The stall holders are always there and because of the way we are placed at different spots, we have become friends with so many of them and they know us by name. Whatever the stage they are at, they are all precious in God's kingdom. I liken it to planting a seed. There is a time for it to germinate, a time for it to grow, be watered, be supported by sticks to make it grow in the right direction, a time to weed, add mulch, and a time to harvest, but when the fruit is ripened, the farmer is out with the sickle to harvest the ripened fruits.

First Corinthians 3:6-9 says, "I have planted, Apollos watered; but God gave the increase. So then, neither is he that planted, nor he that watered is anything but God that gives the increase.

Now he who plants, and he who waters are one, and each one will receive his reward according to his own labour. For we are God's fellow workers; we are God's field, we are God's building."

I remember going on a mission trip to Athens and we shared the word of God with this Muslim gentleman, and when we asked him if he would like to accept Jesus Christ as his Lord and Saviour, he told us he was ready straight away, because as he said, he had been reading a Bible given to him by a group of Christians he met in Egypt. Then on another occasion, he met another Christian in South Africa, but on that warm sunny day in Athens, salvation was explained in such a way that he could understand and he accepted Christ when we prayed for him. For us, he was a ready fruit because other people had sown and watered the seed already and all we did was harvest it.

On another occasion in Bescot Market, a young man from Ireland just walked straight up to our table, we had a brief chat with him, and he said he was ready to make a commitment because he had been desiring to give his life to Jesus but did not know how. We prayed for him and he received Jesus Christ as his Lord and Saviour. So, let me encourage us all, to tell our salvation stories, share our testimonies, be a blessing and be kind to people. What we are doing is scattering seeds that will one day become a ripened fruit for the kingdom of God if they fall on the fertile soil of the heart. Being a witness in the marketplace makes us hungry for more, especially when we know that people's lives will be changed, transformed, renewed forever.

This is in accordance with what the scripture tells us in Matthew 28:18-20 when Jesus came and spoke to HIS disciples saying, "All authority has been given to me in heaven and on earth. Go therefore and make disciples of all nations, baptising them in the name of the Father and of the Son and of the Holy Spirit, teaching them to observe all things that I have commanded you; and lo, I am with you always, even to the end of the age Amen." That says it all. When we step out in faith to share the love of Jesus to our world, we go with authority because we have been sent and we have the backing of the host heaven.

CHAPTER SEVEN

STORIES FROM THE MARKETPLACE

When we obey the word of God, results always follow. In the gospel of Mark, 16:15-20, Jesus spoke to HIS disciples after HE was resurrected, and HE said to them:

> *Go into all the world and preach the Good News to everyone. Anyone who believes and is baptized will be saved. But anyone who refuses to believe will be condemned. These miraculous signs will accompany those who believe: They will cast out demons in my name, and they will speak in new languages. They will be able to handle snakes with safety, and if they drink anything poisonous, it won't hurt them. They will be able to place their hands on the sick, and they will be healed.*

Mark 16:15-18 NLT

We have the mandate of heaven to go and talk about the love of Christ, and in verse 20 it says, "And they went out and preached everywhere, the Lord working with them and confirming the word through the accompanying signs." When we go to the market, we are there to represent Jesus Christ and HIM crucified.

It is not about church, race, colour, or social status, but about the kingdom of God. We have authority in the name of Jesus and HE is working with us and confirming the Word with accompanying signs. We are partnering with HIM, so when people receive us, they receive Jesus and when they reject us, they reject Jesus because it is about HIM who sent us.

When I got this revelation, I felt a weight lift off me. No one is monitoring what we do, but we are still accountable for how we do what HE has sent us to do.

When we are speaking the truth in righteousness, testimonies take place and there are countless testimonies, but only a few will be mentioned because of space and time.

Since we started at Bescot Market, we have seen so many people accept Jesus Christ as their Lord and Saviour, with people speaking in tongues. This is exciting and at the same time fulfilling. If heaven rejoices when one sinner repents, then who are we not to rejoice and celebrate that one who has found a new life in Christ? It has to be said that certain people will listen and prefer to go away and reflect on what they have heard rather than decide straight away, and that is perfectly fine. Others will take the materials with them to read through later in their own homes. We have had a few of them come back to tell us they read the leaflet and prayed the prayer at the end, which means they have decided to follow Jesus. Such was the case with one of the traders who did not have time to chat with us because of shoppers around his table.

When he saw us few weeks later, he ran to our stall excited, and was shouting, "I prayed the prayer, I prayed the prayer, I prayed the prayer on the back of the leaflet you gave me and I felt different, a sense of peace, and I have had joy in my heart ever since!" We have had many of such people and what we do at this point is to give them a copy of a New Testament Bible and encourage them to begin to attend a local Church. This we did for many years, and during one of my course correction moments I had a burden in my heart, and then I realised that we have been making converts and not disciples. I will elaborate on this later in this book.

We met a lady with chronic back pain who came to shop with her husband and son. When she came to our table and we began to chat, she told us that she had been in so much pain that she could not carry her son. We prayed for her and she accepted Christ as her Lord and Saviour. At the same time, her back was healed instantly and as a confirmation of her healing, she lifted her son with ease, something she had not been able to do for years. Thank you, Jesus!

During one of our outings, we saw two Muslim women with their children in the market, window shopping. We offered balloons to them and one of the boys told us that his brother could not speak nor hear and he had been that way since he was little. We asked his mother whether we could pray for him but as the mother was contemplating, her older son held his brother's hands and brought him to us. I remember Patricia Chang, one of our team members praying for the little boy, while the rest of us stood in agreement. We noticed the little boy smile and she asked him to shout "Jesus!" and he shouted Jesus several times. She also clapped in his ears, and he heard.

We were all amazed, rejoicing and thanking God, and so was the little boy and his brother but their mother, surprisingly, began to panic, and they hurried out of our stall (our stand or booth in the market). We were all shocked that she could not rejoice that God had healed her son. However, we found out that when she got home, she was going to have to explain what had happened and that was why she panicked. How sad that people should continue to live in bondage and not be free to accept the gift of what Jesus had already paid for. The irony of this case was that, after she hurriedly left our stall with her sons, she came back to collect more balloons for other children in her family. These balloons had 'Smile, Jesus is Lord' inscribed on them, we gave her as many as she wanted. More seeds were sown, because as people read those words, they will be declaring that Jesus is Lord.

The same day, we had an eleven-year-old boy, called "J", walk up to our table willingly, and I began to interact with him. He asked for a balloon and took some postcards to read and to send to his grandmother who he said was a Christian. This was to be the beginning of an eleven-year journey with him, and still counting, because he kept coming back whenever he saw a trail of balloons, letting him know that we were around.

He accompanied his dad, who is one of the traders, to the market, so whenever we were around, our stall became his favourite place to go to when he took a break from helping his dad. He accepted Christ as his Saviour and we got to meet his father. He would come and talk to us about school and how he was bullied because of his newfound faith and so on. We continued to disciple him until he finished secondary school and was ready to further his education.

It was not just him. There were other children as well who would hang out with us, with the permission of their parents, and they too received Christ. One of them, that I will call "Lily" for confidential purposes, came with her mother and after we shared the gospel with her, she gave her life to Jesus and was so happy and could not stop smiling.

It was coming up to Christmas this particular year and a man came to our stall looking so lost. When we began to interact with him, he opened up to us, telling us that he was not looking forward to Christmas. He had lost his wife and was wearing a chain with a locket which contained her ashes. He was obviously emotionally wounded, but as we began to share the love of Christ with him, he surrendered to Jesus and accepted HIM as the Lord of his life. The joy of seeing people's faces light up when this happens is priceless.

One of the unwelcoming traders we had met had a partner who worked with him. His partner was more receptive, and most times we would be allocated a table next to them. We began talking to them, and gradually, things began to change. The one who was receptive would listen to us as we shared the scriptures with him but the other would not. On this particular day, he called me over and said he had something to tell me. He began to explain to me the experience he had a few nights before. He had gone to bed that night and when he woke up, he noticed that his ring was not on his finger but on the bed.

He thought long and hard about how on earth the ring had left his finger and was now on the bed. He said he took it and put it back on his finger, and when it was time for bed, he went to sleep, only to notice that the ring was on the bed again and not on his finger.

He said his reaction was one of fear initially, but he picked up the ring and was about to put it back on the same finger, but felt restrained to do so. For the first time in many years, he decided not to wear that ring and things began to change for him. He could only attribute this experience to the conversation I had had with him about giving his life to Jesus. The story behind that ring was that he had gone to a local market with his friend, and both had bought the same ring. However, since then things had started going really bad for him. He had encountered one challenge after another, and at one point he was beaten up and left to die, but was thankfully found by a good Samaritan who took him to hospital.

After his recovery, his future dreams were shattered, and he was placed on benefits to help him find his feet again. It was at this point that he started coming to the market with his friend to support him and earn some money to help provide his basic needs. As a result of Christ in his life, this young man was delivered from some demonic influences that he did not even know about. He began to pray and went back to church, and it was not long after this encounter that he stopped trading on a Sunday, and has moved on since.

We had a few other traders who had stopped trading on Sundays and had gone back to church. I caught up with some of them and one said that, as a follower of Jesus, he felt bad seeing us in the market sharing the gospel while he was there trading to make money. So, he decided to return to church and serve there on Sunday mornings by helping to set up for the worship team.

He was using his skills as an electrician for the lighting and multimedia support. When he did that, he said his relationship with God grew stronger, he had more time for his family, and his income increased greatly. God blessed his business and he was making more from six days of trading than he had done from seven days, including the Sunday market. The other gentleman decided to attend his church service first, before coming, and soon he was making more than he did if he traded all day.

The testimonies from the traders were heart-warming. As we prayer walked around, we came across traders who were new in the market and just starting off with their businesses. We would pray for their businesses to prosper, and they saw significant growth in what they did. One of them testified that when he first started with his wife, they were struggling. They did not make many sales, but after we were positioned near them one Sunday, and we prayed for them, things changed. Their business grew so much that they had to have two stalls to trade from each time. When we met them again, they gave the testimony that they too had made connection with their church again, and one of them had got baptised and their faith in Jesus had grown stronger.

God was also touching and blessing Christians who came to Bescot Market on their way back from church. Some of them would come and collect materials to start up some small groups in their area, and they would come back for resources to maintain those groups and ask questions about how we started.

We receive a lot of encouragement from Christians who thank us for being bold to stand and do what we do. One of such people went ahead to start a similar outreach in their area and she was doing well the last time we caught up with her.

God is really blessing people in the market. It is not just the shoppers and the traders; even the market team have been tremendously blessed. When we started, the market manager and his team were involved with just two sites, but a few years later there has been a proliferation of markets in the area and we have been invited to do there exactly what we do in Bescot, although due to our limited capacity, we haven't been able to do so.

The partnership with the market team has been incredible. The favour we receive is at another level, as the Bible puts it "favour upon favour, grace upon grace." The Market Manager would ring us and pass on prayer requests to pray for the traders or their families when they were in hospital or undergoing surgery. One such occasion was for an eight-year-old girl scheduled for high-risk cardiac surgery and whose her mother was very concerned. We prayed for her by liaising with her mother. The surgery was successful and today the girl is nineteen years old and about to start her university education.

Another case was for a premature baby who was in an incubator for months and whose parents were told by the doctors that he had a fifty-fifty chance of survival and if he did pull through, he would end up with abnormalities. This baby was the first child of a wonderful couple and had been born after twelve years of marriage. We got our church involved and we prayed.

Eighteen months later, we saw him with his parents in the market looking very healthy and living a normal life with no complications whatsoever.

Awesome God, thank you. Other people dropped by for guidance, comfort, encouragement, prayers, and as mentioned earlier, some came to be resourced, even university students. What an awesome God we serve and who would not want to know and serve our ever-living God?

We do have a good laugh when some people tried to dodge going to their church, and then bump into us in the marketplace. They come and confess that they were meant to be in church but for some reason decided to come to the market for a quick pick up of various items. They always say that God has a good sense of humour because he was also waiting for them in the marketplace. But we know better that our loving Father is not keeping a register of who goes to church and who does not. We always end up having a time of fellowship with them and sometimes praying for each other.

Do not be deceived by people's outward appearance, because behind those layers of clothing are spiritually hungry, thirsty and impoverished souls seeking to be loved and refreshed by the Most High God. One such person was a lady who came to the market with her children. She spoke to the children in their language and asked them to come to us and collect some balloons, lollies, as well as leaflets which we did not hesitate to give but we thought it was unusual for children that age to wander about in the market without an adult, so we asked them where their mother was? Unknown to us, she was in the next stall watching and listening to our conversation. At this point, she came over to our stall and began to ask questions about how she could become a Christian. She was hiding because of her clothing and what she represented, but she said she could not hide anymore.

She told us how her friend had become a Christian, and how she had watched her change into a new woman, and she had wanted what her friend had. She could speak English, so we took our time investing the word of God into her life, and what was amazing was that her children also listened. When we had finished sharing the scriptures, we asked her whether she wanted to receive Jesus as her Lord and Saviour and it was a resounding yes. In the middle of the market, both she and her children received Jesus Christ into their lives. It was a beautiful sight to behold, the salvation of a household there in the market. It is a testament to the way we live when others so easily want to know Christ. We just need to live well so that we can impact lives. I thank God for this lady's friend who made such a positive impact on her life to the extent that when she saw an opportunity, she was not going to miss it. Thank God she didn't. They went home rejoicing.

CHAPTER EIGHT

THERE ARE MANY ADVERSARIES

During our preparation period of waiting, the Holy Spirit had clearly told me that "a great and effective door had been opened unto us but there were many adversaries." We were aware that challenges would come. One thing Jesus said to HIS disciples when he sent them out to make disciples of all men was that HE would be with them always, even unto the end of the age. The same applies to us. It was important for us to know this. HE did not send us to argue, debate, condemn or fight with anyone. HE sent us out to love. This is important for everyone to understand, that Jesus is not asking us to judge but to share the good news of what HE did for us on Calvary. Just tell the story. The truth they hear and know, that is what will set them free. The nature of God is love, and we need to always remember this. It is difficult sometimes because even when we show love, certain people are there to resist, ridicule, challenge, and discredit what you do. We must remember that the devil, from the start, has been out to steal, kill and destroy, but thank God for the gift of Jesus who came that we might have life and have it to the full. HE came to seek and save the lost.

In John 3:17, it says "For God sent not HIS Son into the world to condemn the world; but that the world through

HIM might be saved." If HE did not condemn anyone, then why should we condemn people? We must understand that when we are hated or persecuted, it is not because of us, but because of HIM who sent us. We have come across stiff opposition on many occasions, and as HE promised, HE was always there and will always be. When the challenging people come, they pretend to be interested and then they want to argue. Some have even told us that we are wasting time. They think that Jesus is not the Son of God, they argue about HIS resurrection. They would agree that Jesus truly died but that HIS resurrection was false because the person who was resurrected was someone who looked like HIM. How sad is this that the devil will deceive people into believing all sorts of lies, and shockingly, people are so gullible to accept them. The resurrection of Jesus is an infallible truth and a defining moment in the history of Christianity.

What Jesus did for mankind should be celebrated and shared. We do not preach religion or church, but we share the love of Jesus and if people want to know more, then we tell them more and if they don't, we bless them still and bid them farewell. First Corinthians 15:12-20 addresses this very well. This is what verses 19-20 say," If in this life only we have hope in Christ, we are of all men the most pitiable. But now Christ is risen from the dead and has become the first fruits of those who have fallen asleep."

Various people have a preconceived idea that religion is bad, and in many ways I agree. Christianity, however, is not about religion but about relationship. Jesus laid down HIS life for sins HE did not commit. HE took our place and that is why HE said in John 3:17 "For God did not send

His Son into the world to condemn the world, but that the world through HIM might be saved."

People need to understand that, and not to blame God when things go wrong in their lives or in the world. God is a good God and wants nothing more than to love us and to have fellowship with us. It is not head knowledge of the bible that matters but heart knowledge of God and doing life with HIM on a daily basis. Some people often say they have read the bible many times and they quote the scriptures completely out of context and come to a wrong conclusion. Such people discourage others around them who truly want to know more and that is disheartening. Sometimes, you can hardly get a word in, as was the case with one gentleman who was always loud, attracting a lot of attention and not allowing us explain things to him.

It is how we live that matter, and not how many scriptures we can quote. Jesus said to HIS disciples in John 13:34-35, "A new commandment I give to you, that you love one another; as I have loved you, that you also love one another. By this all will know that you are My disciples, if you have love one for another." We are there to love them even when they are unlovable. We befriend them and share with them the good news, and we are truly not ashamed of the gospel of Jesus Christ for it is the power of God unto salvation.

We come across people who walk up to us and ask why we are spreading the white-man's religion. They would argue that Jesus was a white man, and the Bible was translated by "the white man." Some of them even say they were raised in church but now they are seeking the gods of their ancestors, leaving this country and emigrating to different parts of the world to worship their own gods.

They are full of hate and so are their words. Others have said they only believe in the Old Testament and not the New Testament. Some are clearly atheists and do not mince words in expressing their thoughts.

Various people are more vocal than the others and they come straight to our stall to rant and challenge us, often asking us questions that result in arguments. We would always remind ourselves of why we are there in the first place, and that is to lift up the name of Jesus and HIM crucified. When we do that, HE will draw all men to HIMSELF. It is very sad that when we talk about God, people listen but the moment you mention the name of Jesus, they react very strangely. This is because of what they have believed in but when they hear the message of the gospel, their views change.

A few people have resorted to mockery. When they feel that we have too much of an influx of people to our stall, they would often belt out "Hallelujah!" thinking that shoppers will be drawn to them, and that they will be able to sell their goods.

Recently, we had an experience of an elderly man who was in the market with a dart board and some darts, inviting people to pay some money and have a go at the game. As I mentioned earlier, we can be positioned anywhere in the market, and on this day, we were set up by his stall. We carried on with our day as usual, and it was not long before I felt a nudge to go over and say hello him. Well, my attempt at friendship was greeted with a complaint and threats because, he said, we were talking to people in front of his stall and stopping them from noticing his business.

Truly, this was not the case because if you are talking to people, sometimes they carry on walking and it is only out of courtesy that you walk alongside them to continue with the conversation because they are in a hurry. It would be rude and strange to ask people to stop in front of your stall and once they move, then you stop talking to them. However, I apologised and advised the ladies to try not to stop in front of his stall when chatting with people.

Before I knew what was happening, he had walked across to the other traders to stir and incite others to gang up against us. The next thing was, he was shouting out loud that we were being insensitive and stopping customers from coming to him. People began to gather, and he went and reported us to one of the market team staff who happened to be walking past at the time.

What the enemy meant for evil, God always turns around for our good. People continued to flock to our stand, and he began to blaspheme, which did not help his business at all. In the twelve years we have been going to Bescot Market, this is the first time ever anyone had complained about us to the market team. When we finished, we went over and said goodbye to him and wished him well.

However, I felt the need to speak to the Market Manager about what had happened, and his first response was, "I knew there was something about that man. He will not come back again." I had to plead on his behalf to say,

"Please let him stay, let him continue to trade," as we did not want him to miss out on that source of income.

There were some other frosty neighbours over the years, but they gradually warmed to us. The Scripture teaches us to love others even when they are unlovable. The Holy Spirit will help us to love them. It is very sad that such things should happen, but I attribute it to a lack of knowledge. We should continue to love them, show them some grace and the Holy Spirit will do the rest. One such frosty neighbour is now one of our most trusted friends who confessed that he felt bad not being in church and not praying as he should. Then he said he decided not to rush out too early to the market but to use that time to read his bible and pray. When he started doing that, things changed for him. He had more peace in himself, and has come to love and welcome us. If we are not there, he will ask about us to check that all is well. Our God is good indeed.

Jesus faced a lot of opposition when HE was on the earth, and instead of fighting back, HE blessed them. He spent a lot of time teaching those who followed HIM and one such teaching was HIS Sermon on the Mount, as recorded in Mathew 5, also known as the Beatitudes. Chapter 5:7-12 says, "Blessed are the merciful: for they shall obtain mercy. Blessed are the pure in heart: for they shall see God. Blessed are the peacemakers: for they shall be called the children of God. Blessed are they which are persecuted for righteousness' sake: for theirs is the Kingdom of heaven. Blessed are you when they revile and persecute you and say all kinds of evil against you falsely for My sake. Rejoice and be exceedingly glad, for great is your reward in heaven, for so they persecuted the prophets who were before you." Christians face adversaries in their service, especially out on the mission field where many are persecuted for sharing the gospel of Jesus Christ.

However, we must continue, because if they persecuted Jesus, we will also be persecuted. We ask for grace to continue loving and sharing the good news to the least and the lost. In Hebrews 13:12-13, "Jesus suffered and died outside the city gate that HE might sanctify and consecrate the people by the shedding of HIS blood outside the city gate. So, let us then go to them that are outside the gate that we might bear HIS shame and reproach." In other words, by identifying with Him.

Blessed are the merciful,
For they shall obtain mercy.

Blessed are the pure in heart,
For they shall see God.

Blessed are the peacemakers,
For they shall be called sons of God.

Blessed are those who are persecuted
for righteousness' sake,
For theirs is the kingdom of heaven.

Blessed are you when they revile and
persecute you, and say all kinds of evil
against you falsely for My sake.

Rejoice and be exceedingly glad, for
great is your reward in heaven, for so
they persecuted the prophets who
were before you.

Matthew 5:7-12NKJV

CHAPTER NINE

OCCUPY TILL I COME

On the 20th of August 2018, I prayed at exactly 09:02am. That's when I felt a gentle nudge in my spirit to get back into the word. I had been reading the bible and had found myself drifting in and out of thoughts, praying and meditating on the problems before me instead of meditating on the word of God. The Holy Spirit nudged me, and immediately I began to read again, and these words jumped out at me: "Till I come." I then thought of "occupy till I come," which was the phrase Jesus used when HE was teaching HIS followers through parables.

Before going into that, however, let us look at what I was reading that day. I was reading from First Timothy 4:13-16, "Till I come, give attention to reading, to exhortation, to doctrine. Do not neglect the gift that is in you, which was given to you by prophecy with laying on of the hands of the eldership. Meditate on these things; give yourself entirely to them, so that your progress may be evident to all. Take heed to yourself and to the doctrine. Continue in them, for in doing this, you will save both yourself and those who hear you." This was Paul's advice to Timothy and to us. God has given each one of us gifts to use for HIS glory. We must not neglect them or take them for granted. For every gift God gives us, there is a measure of grace to go with it, that it will be not just for our profit but also to bless the people around us. Whatever our gifts are, we ought to put them to good use because a day of reckoning will come when we will give an account of that gift or talent that was given to us In Luke chapter 19:11-26, Jesus used a parable to teach HIS followers, as was His manner during HIS time, and I would like to paraphrase it. HE told them of a certain nobleman who called ten of his servants and gave them ten minas, which is equivalent to ten pounds of silver, and said to them, 'occupy till I come,' or, 'invest this for me while I am away to receive for myself a kingdom.' But his servants hated him, saying he was an austere man, and they did not want him to reign over them.

So it was that when the man came back after he had received his Kingdom. He called his servants to whom he had given the money to give account so that he would know how much every man had gained. The first one said to the nobleman, "Master, your mina has earned you ten minas."

The nobleman said to him, "Well done, good servant; because you were faithful in very little, have authority over ten cities." And the second servant gave his master five minas in return, and he, too, was given authority over five cities.

The third servant came and said to his master, "Here is your mina, which I had put away in a handkerchief, because I feared you, seeing you were an austere man. You collect what you did not deposit and reap where you did not sow." And his master said to him that by the words of his own mouth, he would be judged and called him a wicked man because since the servant thought that of his master, he could have given him his money back, which he would have put in the bank to yield him some interest. He commanded them to take the money from him and give it to the servant who had gained ten minas for his master.

The master went on to say that to everyone who had, more would be given, and of those who did not have, even what they had would be taken from them. The talents and gifts given to us by God are not for show or exhibition but for the furtherance of HIS Kingdom by using them to equip others and bring glory to God.

When our God-given gift is used and put to work, it will produce fruits of righteousness in many. Do not let pride, ego, fear of failure, desires of the flesh, slothfulness and so on stop you. Jesus, our Master, is coming back for HIS church. Are you ready to give HIM a good account, or are you going to tie up or bury your gift because of a wrong someone did to you? Jesus is returning for a Church without walls, not brick and mortar. It is not about which church you go to but about what you have done for HIS Kingdom.

Wherever we go, Jesus goes because HE lives in us and HE said, "I am with you always, even unto the end of the age," Matthew 28:20b. Do not say, 'Little old me, what difference can I make?' Remember, there is a gift in everyone with a measure of grace and faith to go with it. You might be the very person who that one soul is waiting for. I thank God I didn't consider my capabilities or allow my flesh to get in the way because that would have meant limiting God and HIS plans for Bescot Market and Walsall at large. God needs to work through us to reach the people and bring them into HIS Kingdom.

We came across a young gentleman in his thirties who had not stepped into a church before, had never heard of the name Jesus except as a swear word, and didn't know that HE had died and had been resurrected. I was almost in tears. He said he knew there was a creator but did not know anything else.

People are searching and they want to know more about life. Jesus said, "Go and make disciples of all nations, baptizing them in the name of the Father and of the Son and of the Holy Spirit, teaching them all things that I have commanded you; and lo, I am with you always, even to the end of the age." The church is out there, not in a building. So, let's go out there that we might bring people into the fold as Jesus said in John chapter 10:16, "And other sheep I have which are not of this fold; them also I must bring, and they will hear My Voice; and there will be one flock and one shepherd."

Will you go for HIM? Romans 10:14 says, "How then shall they call on HIM in whom they have not believed? And how shall they believe in HIM of whom they have not heard? And how shall they hear without a preacher? And how shall they preach unless they are sent?" We need to go out and shine the light for others to see. Staying in one place and doing church will not do it. I must confess that there are times when I just want to drive straight to church and enjoy fellowship and listen to the word of God being preached and that is beautiful. Still, when I remember what HE has called me to do, I will encourage myself and join the team in the market. Often, a great harvest of souls and blessings will be the result.

There is a place (as in position) for the church to be gathered in a building and a place for the church to be "out there", whatever place "there" might mean for each person, not necessarily in the market. When we partner with the Holy Spirit in obedience, the joy that follows can be very overwhelming. On several occasions, I have turned up at the market to evangelise feeling very tired; the moment I step onto the ground and begin interacting with people, a wave of joy and peace always floods my heart.

This is not just my testimony but other team members experience the same. I dreamt sometime in 2019 that I was attending a church conference. I stepped out of the hall and was chatting with one of my church elders when I looked up and there in the sky, I saw these words clearly written: "I send you, Go." The word Go had a capital G. When I woke up and pondered over it, I knew I was in the right place doing what HE wants me to do until HE reveals another plan for me, which I know HE will make plain in due time. It is very fulfilling to know that we are exactly where God wants us to be and doing what HE wants us to do.

On the 17th of January 2019, I was in a dream and Psalm 139 was being read out and as I listened and looked on, the Lord showed me the map of the United Kingdom. As I continued to listen, a strong beam of light shone all over the map and the light began to travel very fast, highlighting boundaries and making a cracking noise which I liken to the sound one hears when hot water is poured into a glass cup and cracks it into pieces.

When I woke up and pondered on it, It was impressed on me that the highlighted boundaries were cities and towns of different sizes. Whatever your location you should pray for your streets, towns, cities and nations. You are the light, and wherever you go, that trail of light follows you. Light illuminates and cannot be hidden, so let us go and shine for others to see.

Darkness cannot comprehend light, so arise and shine, for your time has come. If Jesus the Good Shepherd left the ninety-nine and went in search of the one sheep that was lost, then so should we. Let us step out of our comfort zones and go and reach the least and the lost of our society.

CHAPTER TEN

COURSE CORRECTION

The Father's Heart Missional Community was going well. It brought light to the marketplace, touching and changing lives through the word of God, healings and deliverances for those in bondage. It expanded and brought growth to the market team and even in our own individual lives. But there was a feeling of hunger that I could not describe. I found myself desiring more, there must be more, and as I prayed, there was a burden on my heart that I couldn't shift.

It soon dawned on me that something was wrong somewhere and that quickly came to light in the place of prayer.

The Lord Jesus told HIS disciples to go and make disciples of all nations. HE did not say to go and make converts, but disciples, and disciples follow the leader or teacher in their teachings and way of life until they become like their teacher.

Discipleship, in the Christian sense, is a process of enabling someone or a group of people to become like Jesus through teaching the word of God and seeing them living it out.

When we look at this picture, then something is wrong somewhere. Remember, we were not experts in evangelism, but the Holy Spirit taught, guided, and led us through and continues to do so because without HIM we can do nothing. I began to ask the Holy Spirit in the place of prayer what we should do.

The demographics in Bescot Market are very varied. People come from other parts of the country to trade and shop, and sometimes we have come across holidaymakers from different parts of the world. These are people from diverse socioeconomic and educational backgrounds and religious points of view. These different strata of people are represented in the market and many of them are unchurched. The exciting news is that Jesus loves them all, and we need divine wisdom and guidance to reach them with the gospel. What we have done during these years, is interact with them, love them, befriend them, lead them to Lord and let them go.

There was no follow-up for the shoppers except if we bumped into them again in the market or elsewhere. So many of them had received Christ as their Saviour and what we had done up to this point was to advise them to go to a Bible-believing church near them to continue their journey as new believers.

Then, we did not see anything wrong with that until this burden came. We were and still are more Kingdom-focused than church-focused, but depending on where they lived, we would signpost them to a church near them, to be followed up.

We did not know whether they were growing in their newfound faith or not, but when the burden came, it became a matter of great concern for me. I shared this with the group and the church leaders then, and the thought was to secure a place in the market where it would be easy for them to stop by for prayers or Bible study. We thought of using our own marquee to offer privacy because some have shied away from prayers either because they do not want to be seen or they would prefer a private setting to talk about their problems.

I approached the Market Manager then, Steve Evans, and he was happy to support us and provide whatever we needed, but he had to discuss this with his boss. After that discussion, the feedback was that we could use part of the office, which Steve and the team cleared and made ready for us. When he showed it to me and the team, we were delighted and grateful for the effort they had put into finding the room for us.

However, because of poor ventilation and because the room was quite small, we could not use it for that purpose. With his permission, though, we used it as a storage space to minimise the lifting and carrying of some of the items we used regularly.

I took this back to the Missional Community Co-ordinator, Mary Banks. After deliberations, the advice was to look for a place to rent for a few hours to start this discipleship class. The logistics were very tricky because there were many things to consider, such as location, accessibility, and convenience of the venue. After all, the landlord must be happy for us to start a small group with the potential of growing into a church if it takes off. There was so much to consider, but while all this was happening, we continued to disciple the traders each time we prayer-walked or set up our stall because they remained in their allocated spot. The friends we had made were always happy to see us and give us progress reports on the issues we had prayed about.

This was the situation until I had the privilege of going to Charis Bible College in Walsall. During my third year, we were asked to present a business pitch for a ministry or business that we were interested in pursuing. This was to be presented to the whole class, and some business experts were invited to critique us and give their feedback. At the end of the presentations, six businesses would be chosen, and the chosen six would be supported by Andrew Wommack Ministries with resources if need be.

When I heard that, my heart leapt for joy. I went home that day and began to pray about it, and I knew God had opened a door of opportunity for us.

This was a church ministry and I also needed to be sure that it would not in any way interfere with the church values. As I prayed about it, I had peace, and I knew it was the right thing to do. I had reached that point where I needed to see more happening in Bescot. There must be more, and in fact, as we prayer walked on one of the occasions, the Lord told us to desire much more. I certainly would not want to limit God in any way. We wanted HIM to have HIS way in the marketplace. All I wanted from this exercise was to learn from others and discover what more we could do to see ground-breaking transformations and miracles in Bescot Market. I took this idea to the team, and we prayed about it. After that, I indicated that I was going to do a presentation. On the day of the class presentations, everyone was there with the business experts and Charis Bible College tutors.

After the presentation from eight different businesses and ministries, six were chosen by the panel and the student votes contributed to the overall decision.

I had a shock when Father's Heart Missional Community was among the first three to be called out. I was excited and thankful to God for this opportunity to network with others, identify any area of growth and discover what it might be that we were not doing right, resulting in what seemed like stagnation, although people were still getting saved.

People showed interest, and we formed a little group called Father's Heart Ministry. I was the leader of the group, and during that exercise, a lot of things came to light because it gave me the opportunity to do some proper planning for the project as if it was a proper business or ministry project.

Experiences were shared by people interested in evangelism, owned their own businesses or ran similar ministries. Because a lot was already being done, it was a question of expanding on what was already in place and building in what was missing without losing the primary purpose of why God sent us there. It was also important to me that what we did would always align with the core five values of my church, the Church at Junction Ten. These values are: that we should have a Servant heart, a Passionate heart, be Grace driven, a Generous heart and a Missional heart. The Father's Heart Missional Community reflects these five core values in the marketplace.

Then, we wrote our mission statement, vision, core focus, five-year plan, and so on. I cannot mention everything we did in this book, but I will most certainly share some of the aspects we developed, which, I am glad to say, are being implemented.

Our mission statement now is to communicate the gospel of Jesus to the people in the marketplace and surroundings through friendship, sharing the love of Christ and investing the Kingdom of God into their hearts when the opportunity arises. This fitted in well with one of our guiding scriptures, which was from Isaiah 58:12, "Those from among you shall build the old waste places; you shall raise up the foundations of many generations; And you shall be called the Repairer of the Breach, The Restorer of Streets to Dwell In."

Our vision has always been to reach the least and the lost with the gospel of Jesus Christ and to disciple them. Discipling them made the great commission in Matthew 28: 18-20 complete for me. I could feel the burden lifted already, just merely by knowing that the Holy Spirit had, through these lovely people, opened our eyes to other ways of achieving our goal without hiring or renting any venue.

A venue for discipleship became more of an issue because our church was in the process of rebuilding, coupled with the facts that I mentioned earlier, like location, accessibility, and people's willingness to commit, but God always makes a way.

We came up with a five-year plan to help us stay focused; this was: To continue to maintain links with the market team and discuss future plans as and when; To invite people who are passionate and willing to join the team and be trained, commitment slip completed to short term or long-term commitment. We wanted to include Christians from other churches who were passionate about soul-winning and discipleship. Some people were happy to join us for a season while others considered being part of the team for the long haul. A bigger team would enable us to stay longer in the market and have more reach. We needed to acquire a marquee to mount in the marketplace and provide privacy for prayers, chats, videos, music, tables, banners and so on.

We were to start a discipleship class twice a month, teach them for about six to eight weeks and then signpost them to Bible-believing churches close to them geographically. We were to extend the Father's Heart Missional Community to other markets and Bescot Stadium without bypassing any protocol and then do a regular course correction every year to evaluate our progress. We had identified our strengths, weaknesses, opportunities and threats to help us build and grow as a ministry. We had planned to advertise the ministry through our church social media platforms like Facebook, church websites, church journals and newsletters, and also by word of mouth. We already had a yearly Christmas special outreach. Still, we had also planned to do two more events with a view to reaching parents and grandparents with the gospel.

We needed some financial support which the church provided, and we have had donations from team members and others who had committed to be financially part of the ministry. May the Lord bless you all immensely for sowing into God's Kingdom. So, with the business model canvas completed, we had our key partners, key resources, key activities, value propositions, customer relationships, channels, customer segments, cost structure and revenue streams in place. We were ready to go.

I was constantly working with my church administrative team and elders for information and support during this project. It was shortly before I could finish my Third Year in Bible College that the COVID-19 pandemic struck, and the lockdown was enforced.

In fact, the rest of the project and the presentation of our business plan were completed virtually.

There were mixed emotions going through my mind and the minds of everyone concerned. Still, honestly, my heart was really yearning to be out there sharing the gospel and telling people about Jesus, who gave everything for us. Outdoor venues, offices and shops were shut, including the market. We could not do anything but continue to study the bible and pray weekly via Zoom, which brought much unity to the team. We have always been like a family, which made us appreciate each other even more.

It was a period to continue to course correct and hear God for the next season. I must point out here that being in Charis Bible College and leading the project was a pivotal time for the journey of this ministry. The space to pray and listen to the Holy Spirit made me take note of that burden to "desire much more" and the boldness to step forward and explore even though I was not preparing for a new business venture.

I stepped out in faith to learn how to grow and make robust what was in place but felt we were at a standstill. We need to be spiritually sensitive to be able to receive guidance and direction in what we were doing especially as we were serving God.

We learn to discern the times and seasons. When to move and when to stop and wait, when to speak and be quiet, what to speak, and when and how to act. Intimacy with God will teach us discernment, give us direction, speed or accelerated results, new strategies, and the blueprint for what HE has planned for us to do. Like the sons of Issachar in the bible, who understood the times and knew what Israel had to do... First Chronicles 12:32. When you have clarity from the Holy Spirit, you move with sagacity because you know that when you step out, the host of heaven is behind you, even when it seems that you do not know what you are doing.

Jesus is always with us, as HE promised, and when we open our mouths, HE will fill them with the right words to speak, in due season, to those who need to hear it. Hallelujah!!

When the lockdown began to ease, we headed out to the market because a lot of people were fearful. We needed to spread the message of hope, love, and encouragement, for God has not given us a spirit of fear but of love, power and sound mind. We started by just prayer walking the market, chatting with people and praying for them. Some had lost loved ones or neighbours and needed to hear a different message. Others had lost businesses, finances, self-worth, and self-esteem was low. The message of hope, love and peace could not have been more highly needed than at such a time. We gave out leaflets as we interacted with people, and shortly after this period, the market opened properly.

However, the optional wearing of masks and hand sanitising continued. We had to think outside the box.

Discipleship was still the main outcome of the course correction, but how were we to implement that when face-to-face meetings were quite limited? The Holy Spirit led us to acquire a phone and use it to reach out to people and to disciple them that way for a start, by ringing them up and offering words of hope and encouragement or by them ringing us for a friendly chat or for prayers or to ask questions about their faith.

The shoppers and traders were asked if they would be happy to be a part of our virtual Bible study group and some of them agreed. Others were referred to us through networking. I got to know a friend during lockdown via our neighbourhood link and she had started an online prayer group that met virtually to pray for our community. She did street evangelism as well and was happy to refer some of their new converts to us for discipleship.

With about fifteen people interested at that time, the Bescot Bible study group was birthed. We have grown to over thirty-five people on the list and we have continued to do virtual Bible studies twice a month. They are only sometimes in attendance but would ring and ask for prayers and advice about their newfound faith or for something else. We have seen some of them grow closer to God and become stronger in their faith. I remember contemplating stopping the virtual study group and the Lord spoke to me very strongly to continue the class even if only one person attends, and it has been a blessing running it with the team. Praise God! When I took the idea to one of the Elders and the Pastor in my church, Rachel Jenkins, she was happy with the plan to acquire a marquee. She made enquiries, and the church got us a marquee for the market, and things were shaping up, and I can say that God is so faithful in many ways.

The marquee allows us to pray for people without being seen by all. Since the lockdown, many things have changed; we do not meet for breakfast and prayer before starting at the market but instead pray on the market ground. We have stopped using balloons and giving mince pies and drinks during our Christmas outreach for the same reason. We have continued to prayerfully adapt to the current culture or trend and what we think is right. We apply wisdom, depending on how the Holy Spirit leads us. HE is our mentor, and the bible is our navigation manual.

CHAPTER ELEVEN

WOUNDED IN THE HOUSE OF GOD

There is a burden in my heart as a result of a particular group of people we meet in Bescot Market. We come across all kinds of people in the market, but I would like to talk about the angry and the wounded. Many people we come across are angry with God and others are angry with the church.

Some people blame God for their misfortunes or their challenges in life. They say they grew up in church, but God abandoned them when their loved ones were sick and dying. Others say, 'If God is there, why do we have so many children suffering and dying from terrible health conditions? What did they do wrong to warrant that level of suffering?' And the questions and blaming continue. This picture portrays God as a wicked and heartless creator, when the truth is that God is love.

First John 4:8 tells us, "HE who does not love does not know God, for God is love." The bible tells us, "God so loved the world that he gave His only begotten Son, that whoever believes in HIM should not perish but have eternal life. For God did not send HIS Son into the world to condemn the world but that the world through Him might be saved," John 3:16-17. Since this is the case, why then would HE turn round and bring evil upon the very people HE died for? It does not make sense.

Romans 5:8 says, "But God demonstrates HIS own love toward us, in that while we were yet sinners, Christ died for us." And verse 10 says, "For if when we were enemies we were reconciled to God through the death of HIS Son, much more, having been reconciled, we shall be saved by HIS life."

When Jesus died for our sins, HE paid with HIS blood for every sickness we will ever face. Whether it has a name or not Christ Jesus paid for it all for it says, "By HIS stripes, we were healed," (Isaiah 53:5, First Peter 2:24). Jesus would not humble Himself and be crucified and then turn and impute sickness to us. The truth is that from the beginning, Satan has had one agenda: to steal, kill and destroy but Jesus came that we might have life and have life to the full. Satan is out to take away our peace, joy, health, wealth and so on.

Our duty is to resist him, and he will flee from us but when people do not know this, their first reaction is to blame God and become angry with Him.

If only people could understand this and draw near to God through Jesus Christ, their eyes would open to the truth. In the book of Psalms 115:16, it says, "The heavens, even the heavens are the LORD's: But the earth has He given to the children of men." The problem is man's and not God's. People see God as the being who is there to supply their needs, whereas all HE wants is to love and fellowship with us.

"Every good and perfect gift is from the Father of Lights, with whom there is no variation or shadow of turning," James 1:17. Simply put, if it's good, it's God. If it's not, it's not God.

The other group of people are those who are Christians but were wounded in the house of God. Some have told us that they grew up, and served in church, but at times in their lives, when they needed help, guidance, and counsel from their pastor, they were neglected, overlooked, and treated as dirt. Some have been accused of things they didn't do, and others say they have been used as servants and without due regard.

This is very unfortunate. When they tried to leave, they were threatened. Some people have told stories of pastors asking about their financial status when they were new members of those churches, and the stories continue. You hear in the news of abuse in the house of God. How sad! All these people have left the church and have vowed not to return, although they will continue to believe in Jesus Christ. Their argument is that the Church of Jesus Christ is not the building but the people. This is true.

However, we should not forsake the assembling of the righteous as is the manner of some. The gathering of the church is extremely important, but when people leave a church and they do not have a community to continue in fellowship with, then it is only a matter of time before their faith starts to grow cold and they draw back.

One of those contacts told me that the mere mention of fellowship puts him off and reminds him of his past.

This is very unfortunate. We have let God down. The very people HE entrusted the church to are the ones causing HIS followers to leave. In the gospel of Luke, 17:1-4, Jesus said to HIS disciples, "It is impossible that no offences should come, but woe to him through whom they do come! It would be better for him if a mill stone were hung around his neck, and he were thrown into the sea, than that he should offend one of these little ones. Take heed to yourselves. If your brother sins against you, rebuke him; and if he repents, forgive him. And if he sins against you seven times in a day and seven times in a day returns to you, saying, 'I repent,' you shall forgive him." Jesus gave us an example of how to care for the flock when he referred to Himself as the Good Shepherd, as recorded in the gospel of John,10: 11-18.

HE gives HIS life for the sheep but a hireling sees the wolf coming and runs away leaving the sheep for the wolf to catch and scatter them. The hireling does not care for the sheep but Jesus the Good Shepherd knows HIS sheep and HE is known by HIS sheep. As God the Father knows the Good Shepherd "Jesus," even so, the Good Shepherd knows HIS sheep. HE knows them by name and they know HIS voice and will not follow a stranger's voice.

In verses 15-16, HE said, "As the Father knows me, even so I know the Father; and I lay down My life for the sheep. And other sheep I have which are not of this fold; them also I must bring, and there will be one flock and one shepherd."

If Jesus, our Good Shepherd, laid down HIS life for HIS sheep, so should we lay down our lives for those in our congregations.

We have been given the grace for every calling, so every true shepherd should care for the flock and not leave or maltreat them. God gives us the grace to love even the unlovable when we see Christ in them and not allow the flesh to get in the way. In another instance, Jesus left the ninety-nine sheep and went in search of the one. That should be the attitude of a shepherd.

There are people out there that need Christ, and these are the ones we must go and reach. Jesus asked Peter the same question three times in the Gospel of John 21:15, "Simon, son of Jonah, do you love me?" Peter answered on each occasion, "Yes, Lord; you know that I love you," and Jesus responded in this order, "Feed My lambs", "Tend My sheep", "Feed My sheep." After this dialogue Jesus said to Peter, "Follow Me."

Every church leader should know that it is a huge responsibility to be in the position they are in. We must crucify the flesh and allow Jesus to lead us through HIS precious Holy Spirit. For those who have decided to leave the church because of an offence, my question to them is, who are you following? Jesus or your church leader?

If anyone offends you, forgive the biblical way, and heal from it. Allow the Holy Spirit to help, but if you decide to bear the hurt and remain wounded, then I must question whether you knew Christ at all. If you love Jesus, forgive, find another healthy church, and grow your faith. Do not remain a wounded soldier. There is always a choice. Stay focused on Jesus Christ and do not be distracted. I speak out of love.

God gives us grace to love the unlovable when we see Christ in them and not allow the flesh to get in the way.

CHAPTER TWELVE

MORE TESTIMONIES FROM
THE MARKETPLACE

God did some amazing things in the lives of people in Bescot Market. During our Christmas outreach in 2018, we offered people warm drinks and mince pies and one of these was a lady in a wheelchair, called Miss "S", for confidentiality purposes. We had a brief conversation and I remember her saying that she was feeling very cold. We served her hot tea and a mince pie, she left. I thought nothing of it until we came back to the market in February 2019 and saw this lady in a wheelchair selling her goods. We greeted her as usual, and asked about her welfare.

She was clearly shivering from the cold, so I offered her my gloves to keep warm, but she declined and said she was still grateful for the cup of tea and mince pie we served her last Christmas. She recognised us straight away, thanking us for the kindness shown her on that cold winter's day in December.

This opened a door for further interaction, and she told us about her health situation and asked us for prayer. She was taking twenty-four different medications because she was being treated for several health problems. We prayed for her and carried on prayer walking. Weeks later, we saw her again in the market, and this time she was walking about and attending to her customers. When she saw us, she was full of smiles, as though her joy knew no bounds, as she began to share her testimony with us. She stated that shortly after we prayed for her, she went to the hospital to see her consultant for a planned appointment.

As she sat and waited for her name to be called, all she could think about was us, and she could see our faces in her mind's eye, praying for her. For eight years, she had waited to be investigated to know the right treatment pathway for her. She needed to be hospitalised for this to happen and had waited for a hospital bed so that she could at least have a diagnosis. Miss S had been treated symptomatically all this while, without relief, but on her visit to the hospital, a bed was available for the investigations to be carried out. When all was done, she was eventually discharged from the hospital with only four medications. The doctor told her that the other twenty medications were unnecessary. Her results were normal. So, she had been receiving treatment for sicknesses she did not have. God healed her, and she was altogether a different woman, walking about without her wheelchair. Praise God!

On another occasion, we met a lady called "V" in the market, selling her goods. She was not very friendly because when we went over to her stall to say hello and offer her some leaflets/tracts, she asked us to give them to those who needed them the most because she was already a Christian. However, when Nwanneka asked whether she needed prayer for anything, she said, "Yes," and consented to be prayed for. When Nwanneka began to pray for her, the Lord gave me a word for her, which was that she was to: "Focus on God, and HE will take care of the rest." After that prayer, I shared this with her, and she confirmed that the word was for her. She began to tell us about her life and business and the challenge she was facing. We blessed her and left.

This happened shortly after the COVID-19 pandemic lockdown was lifted. We did not want to have a stall immediately because of the logistics involved, and even though we had acquired our marquee at this time, we still did not feel led to start putting the tables out. So, all we could safely do now was to prayer walk and offer pastoral care in this way. Some of the traders had COVID-19 themselves and others had lost family and friends to the same. The next time we saw Miss V she was smiling, and told us how she sold all her goods the day we prayed for her and asked for prayers again. She called me when I got home later requesting more prayer because of the pain in her back. When she got healed, she called again for more prayer concerning her work and other things, and this became a regular thing. God turned things around for her and she has gone on to share her testimony with many people.

She has referred many people to us. These people have given their lives to the Lord over the phone, and we have continued to disciple them. Miss 'V's faith in the Lord was also stirred up because she went about praying for many people with back problems and they were getting healed.

Also, some women who desired to have children conceived and delivered safely after she prayed for them. Her business blossomed and now she needs at least two tables to display her goods each time. Our God is faithful indeed. She is one of the committed, regular attendees to the discipleship class we hold for our Bescot friends. God turned things around for her and now she is prospering and always smiling. Hallelujah!

There was a day we were in the market and ministering to people, when a lady walked past with her Zimmer frame, clearly struggling to walk. Seeing this, we asked her if she wanted to be prayed for. Upon her consent, we prayed for her, and she was about to leave when we asked whether she had received Christ as her Saviour? She said no. So, we prayed for her to receive Jesus Christ into her life and also asked the Holy Spirit to come upon her. Immediately, she began to exclaim, "I feel different, I feel different!" so we asked her what happened? She testified that she felt a weight lift off her and she felt light in herself. She was happy and smiling and carried her walking frame as she left our stall. The Holy Spirit's wonderful power touched her and freed her from her multiple health conditions. Praise God!

During the economic crunch about a decade ago, some of the shops in the retail park area closed down because people stopped trading. As we prayer walked, we would stand in front of those shops and pray that things would change, and that these shops would be opened. We saw God answer those prayers and the area buzzed again, although things are different today. It made me realise that no matter how bad things may appear, our prayers change things, so we cannot afford to be quiet and feel miserable and overwhelmed when things go wrong. We can make a difference through our prayers. The bible tells us that the effectual fervent prayer of a righteous man avails much. With our prayers, we effect changes in our world.

It reminds me of the prophet Elijah in the scripture, who prayed and there was no rain in Israel for three and a half years. He prayed again and the heavens gave rain.

Let us be encouraged; our prayers can change the course of action in the destiny of people, cities, and nations. It reminds me also of what the prophet Elisha said to the King of Israel during a time of famine.

There was famine in the land and people were suffering and could barely eat. It was so bad that people were eating bird dung and even boiling and eating their children. The King of Israel then was very concerned and came to the man of God Elisha, very angry, and threatening to kill him, but Elisha said to him, in 2nd Kings 7:1-2, "Hear the word of the Lord. Thus says the Lord: tomorrow about this time a seah (unit of dry measure used amongst the Jews) of fine flour shall be sold for a shekel, and two seahs of barley for a shekel, at the gate of Samaria." So, an officer in the King's entourage responded and said, "If the Lord would make windows in heaven, could this thing be?" Elisha said to him, "In fact, you shall see it with your eyes, but shall not eat of it." The King's man doubted God, and when you read the rest of the story in Second Kings, Chapter seven, the turn round happened exactly the way Elisha had said it because God caused the Syrians to hear the noise of chariots and horses and they fled from their homes leaving behind food, clothing and so on.

Then four lepers decided to go into the Syrian camp and surrender to the army so that they could at least have food to eat, and when they got to the camp, it was deserted. Instead of surrendering, they found so much food, clothing, silver and gold in this season of scarcity that they had their fill. They alerted the King and the other Israelites who, when they arrived the scene, found feasts laid out everywhere but abandoned in haste by the Syrians when they heard the noise and thought the king of Israel had hired the Egyptian army to attack them. With so much food everywhere, the king appointed the officer who had doubted Elisha to take charge of the gate, but unfortunately for him, he was trampled and died. The word of Elisha the prophet came to pass.

There is nothing our God cannot do for HIS followers. HE has also empowered us in that we can declare things in faith, and they come to pass. With this in mind, we can speak to dead businesses, situations, and even failing health and see changes take place. We should never doubt what God can do and in Bescot, we believe HIM for so much more.

There is a man I call Mr. P who used to come to the market to beg for money. He would sit by the road on a sheet of cardboard and beg. He had no fixed address and was content just sitting with his notice, waiting for someone to show him some kindness. When we saw him, he was quite receptive but did not say much.

As time went by though, we got to know him better. He had suffered an industrial injury which took some of his fingers, making it difficult for him to grab and hold certain things for long. He always wore gloves and as we continued to visit him whenever we were in the market, the conversation became friendlier, and he was open to us. He had been in the church choir as a young lad and served God in that way, but when his mother died, he had a disagreement with the church over his mother's funeral and that was how he stopped going to church. As he grew older, he became quite distanced from the church.

Although we invited him to church, we knew it was going to be hard for him, so what we did was to go and see him each time we were there and ask about his welfare.

One day, I asked him if I could read him some scriptures and he said yes. So, each visit we would stop by to see Mr. P and read the bible to him because he said he couldn't read, and we would usually bless him in other ways while we were there. This went on for a couple of years until one day, we saw Mr. P in the market, walking about chatting and greeting people. We never saw him again because he moved on. I thank God for the opportunity to share scriptures with him regularly for that length of time and I pray that those seeds will bear fruit one day and bring him closer to the community of Christians again. I was very happy that he forgave those who offended him in church. Praise God!

I believe we will never really know the impact Father's Heart Missional Community and other similar ministries make in people's lives until we get to heaven when we are called home.

*Let us be encouraged ...
our prayers can change
the course of action in
the destiny of people,
cities and nations.*

CHAPTER THIRTEEN

HE OPENED MY EYES

I woke up one Sunday morning and laid in bed, thinking about Bescot, when the Lord opened my eyes and I literally saw the heavens open and a piercing light shone through. As I looked on, a white bird, which I assumed to be a dove, flew out through the piercing light, and I snapped out of it. It was quite a sight! I began to ponder about the picture I had just seen and knew immediately that God had gone ahead of us. I shared this with the team when we met up in Bescot that morning, and we prayed about it. I will forever remember it; we went on to have a beautiful and fruitful day.

When God opens our eyes, it gives us reassurance and confidence that HE is with us just like HE promised. HE never forsakes HIS own. HE is always with us, confirming HIS word. HE has given me so many dreams about Bescot Market, and these have been a great help and guide in decision-making.

I was in a dream one night and Patricia, Juliet and I were walking past the Bescot Market and chatting. When we got exactly in front of the market Juliet brought out a white paper tissue which did not look particularly clean and placed it on the lips of a dumb woman who was also in the vicinity. My first thought was, why would she place a rumpled tissue paper from her pocket on this woman's mouth, but as I was wondering where she was going with this, the lady began to speak and was joyful. We were all surprised and happy then Patricia said, "I knew she was going to do that." I was amazed that the miracle had taken place right in front of the market.

We continued walking and chatting ending up at Charis Bible College. When we arrived, a long line of people was waiting to register, and we lined up. As I stood there waiting, a young man walked up and handed me a folder with an unusually long pen with a green ribbon. I was in Bible College at this time, and I recall being in college on the following Saturday. There was a long line of people waiting to register. It was my second year. However, I did not understand the longer-than-normal pen with the green decorative ribbon tied around it that was given to me. It was not until I had written my first book that that dream came to me. That was a God-incidence. HE was giving me a hint of what was to come, but I did not get it until a few years later. I know for sure that there will be many more testimonies from the marketplace to share. May that pen not run dry in Jesus's name. Amen!

Being in Bescot has been such a big learning curve for me and has caused me to depend so much more on the Holy Spirit for guidance and direction. It is reassuring to know that you are in the will of God and serving where HE wants you. On the 16th of March 2013, which was earlier on in this ministry, I had a dream, and in that dream, a little boy of about nine to ten years old ran up to me and asked me where he could have his blood pressure checked. I led him through a long corridor that ran parallel to the road.

As we approached the exit, I realised that the staff checking blood pressures were not there anymore, so we were walking right back when I looked through the door and saw a lady with a stethoscope and blood pressure apparatus; So, I told the lad, look you can get your blood pressure checked there." I noticed at this point that there were different clusters of people doing different activities. When the boy ran off to be checked, I carried on walking down the street and leapt into the air with joy and said out loud, "Thank you Jesus," and at that instant, I noticed a man clothed in a long white robe with a band around his waist, and long hair, he nodded when I said, "Thank you Jesus." Now, I realised that he was among several other groups at the same time. "Awesome!!!" That got me thinking as I carried on walking. A group of ladies were chatting and I asked them for directions. One of them told me to always check where I was going before setting off on my journey.

When I woke up, this thought came to mind: HE was with me, and at the same time with every other group out there. Jesus is omnipresent, omniscient, and omnipotent. HE is everywhere at the same time, and HE answers all our prayers when we call on HIM. All power belongs to HIM; what's more HE is all-knowing. Revelation 19:6 says, "And I heard the voice of a great multitude, and as the voice of mighty thundering, saying, Alleluia: for the Lord God omnipotent reigns!"

Wherever you are located, just tell the story of what Jesus did for you and how you accepted HIM into your life. HE will always be with you as well as with everyone else who believes in HIM all at the same time. HE is the silent listener to every conversation, although we may not see HIM with our physical eyes. Praise God!

I remember one quiet Sunday morning; we turned up at Bescot Market and realised that the market was closed. There were only a few traders about and they were packing up to go because the Police were also in the market. It had rained so heavily the night before that it had led to road closures due to flooding. The drains were spilling over with debris, but because we had planned to prayer walk that day, we carried on as planned while the market admin team and Police also carried on with their own activities. We walked past a drain with a broken concrete slab next to it that had caved in a little bit, and immediately the Lord spoke to me. HE said, "Pray for the broken hearted." I shared it with Bukky who was with me that day, and we began to pray for traders who were going through challenging times in their lives due to sickness, bereavement, problems with finances or life in general. It might seem trivial, but we must be sensitive to the voice of the Holy Spirit and HIS promptings. I could go on and on, but the point I am trying to make here is the importance of intimacy with the Spirit of God and allowing HIM to guide and direct our affairs. Remember, we are co-labourers in HIS vineyard. "For we are God's fellow workers; you are God's field, you are God's building," First Corinthians 3:9 and "He is the Lord of the harvest," Matthew 9:38.

I finish this chapter with what God showed me in March 2011. I saw people of all ages, races and colours holding hands in the sky, floating and spreading in all directions. They were like skydivers but with many more people involved, and the number grew as I continued. This picture signifies unity and diversity. If we are to move forward in anything that God is calling us to do, we must be united in purpose so that we can run with our vision.

In the Christian world today, there is a lot of division and misunderstanding and we have veered away from what God is calling us to do. If we are divided, how can we stand? We have left the most important thing Jesus asked us to do and are spending our time chasing after trivial things. As I sat in church two months later, I remembered this picture again. I thought about the sick in our world, those going through challenging situations, and the need for Christians to be out there ministering to them and praying for them. Being a nurse has also helped me to observe and feel compassion for people around me and stand with them in prayer.

I recall a dream I had that week where I found myself in a place that resembled a garden centre. I was looking around and admiring a variety of plants. There were so many of them: some of them climbing plants, some pot plants, some in the soil, all at different stages of growth. Some of those that were in the pots were ready for transplanting others were in full bloom, while others had green foliage and looked lush. A few of them were drying out and the soil around them was caked, as if in need of some tender loving care.

This got me thinking, why were some plants dried up and dying while others were doing so well? I believe this is a picture of life. Different people at different stages in life, some flourishing and others really struggling, or somewhere in the middle. Wherever and whatever we do in life, let us reach out to people around us who are going through hard times and show them compassion. If we are at the peak of life, let us also remember that those in the valley of life were once on the mountaintop.

We must learn to love others as Christ has loved us, for by this shall all know that we are HIS disciples. The younger people need nurturing and guidance, the older ones who have so much to offer, need to be cared for. Life can often be like a garden centre. Care for it well and it will grow and blossom; but neglect it, and it will wither and die. So, as we have the opportunity, let us do good to all men, especially to the faithful. The Heart of the Father is love.

CHAPTER FOURTEEN

MEET THE TEAM

What we do in the market makes us very visible to the world out there, but we are not alone. The host of heaven is with us always. Yes, we know that, because without the Holy Spirit, we can do nothing. However, this is not the kind of ministry where you operate alone. When Jesus sent HIS disciples, as recorded in the gospels, he sent them out two by two. Let us look at Luke 10:1-2, "After these things the Lord appointed seventy others also, and sent them two by two before HIS face into every city and place where HE Himself was about to go. Then HE said to them, "The harvest is truly great, but the labourers are few; therefore, pray the Lord of the harvest to send out labourers into HIS harvest."

This was also one of the instructions we had received earlier on, and we kept to that. We need each other when we are out there in our communities for support and encouragement. We need to be watchful while ministering or witnessing to people, especially when praying for them. This has been a key point of reference for us and has brought us together. In our team, we all do one demanding job after another. There are bound to be moments of fatigue from the week's workload, even before we get to the market. Still, one thing we have noticed is that the moment we set our feet on the market's ground, we are filled with buzz and excitement. We arrive tired and leave energized. It must be God supplying us with supernatural strength. When we started Father's Heart Ministry, as I mentioned earlier on in chapter four of this book, we were just hungry and ready to serve; we were available and willing to learn. Some people in the team had pockets of knowledge but we were not experts. However, the Holy Spirit, our teacher, prepared us and got us ready. We are still learning from HIM and from one another. We grew to about sixteen people and could run two sessions or split into two groups for a short while. One group at the stall ministering to people, the other group prayer walking the market, and we would swap over at some point. It was a lot of fun. Of all those that started at that time, one couple went on to start a prison ministry, another person emigrated to the Philippines to be a missionary, another joined a different church to support a healing ministry a few withdrew because they were supporting another ministry and two were promoted to glory, my beloved husband being one of them.

Father's Heart made it possible for people to gain experience and grow in confidence to do what God had called them to do, which for me, is a huge blessing. The rest of us are still in the Lord's vineyard and enjoying every bit of it. We have had a few more join us from other churches too.

I have, in the past, led groups of people in my church as well as other Christian organisations, but these were nothing to do with evangelism. So, although I had the revelation and passion for evangelism, I had no experience. However, my attitude was, I will do this even if I make a fool of myself because the vision was beyond me, and I knew that HE who had sent me was able. On the other hand, I am happy that I knew little or nothing about mission so that our dependency would not be on me, or us, but on the one who sent us. It was a total reliance, and as Christians, we should know how to recognise a helper of destiny when we see one. I saw one in the person of Mrs Mary Banks, the J10 Co-ordinator for Missional Communities. Mary was there from the start. She didn't just give us instructions, no, she did the work with us, and she accompanied us to the market for a few years. She was not there on every visit but she was there with us on a regular basis because she had to allow us time to grow as well.

As the Missional Community Coordinator, she organised huddles (friendly meetings) for us on a regular basis, and I was privileged to be a part of her group with some other Missional Community leaders, with whom we had a lot of fun.

In those meetings, we had the space to share our experiences with others and be encouraged. It was also good to have someone hold us accountable for the team we were leading. She helped us to source some of the things we needed at the time and her role in this was priceless. She encouraged us Missional Community Leaders to work together and that was a bonus. That was how we came to work with the worship team and 'Living Waters' Cafe Missional Community. I recall Mary preaching openly in the market on a snowy morning, with a microphone and live worship. It was an awesome outreach. Every ministry needs a "Mary." Well, things happen and there are different seasons in life, and Mary moved on to other things in Church.

I have to say that when the Elders, Rachel Jenkins, Kevin Davis, and Joe Clark, took over the church leadership, the financial support from our church became regular and we had a budget. That was another significant phase in this ministry. Because we evaluate and we course correct from time to time, we have come to find out which leaflets(tracts) and other items for the stall work best for us. The demand for materials in other languages grew and we responded appropriately to meet the need of that population of shoppers. The church admin department began to order the materials for us when we needed them, and that partnership is invaluable.

I would like to mention here that a team from 'Good News for Everyone' (formerly known as Gideons), led by Robert and Debbie Read joined forces with us during several of our Christmas outreach events in Bescot Market, and that was a great partnership.

For everyone who works tirelessly behind the scenes to help us continue to go out there to share the gospel of Jesus Christ, I pray the Lord who sees in secret will reward you openly. In First Samuel 30, it was recorded how David had returned from war with his soldiers dancing and rejoicing, and with so much wealth, having defeated the Philistines. When they got home, they discovered that their wives, children, and livestock had been taken and their homes set alight by the Amalekites. David's soldiers were angry and wanted to stone him, their Captain who had taken them to war. However, David enquired of the Lord, who told him, "Pursue, for you shall surely overtake them and without fail, recover all." However, some of the soldiers were tired and could not carry on to fight another war; David allowed them to stay and guard the wealth they had brought back.

They did pursue and fought the Amalekites, and recovered all, just as the Lord had told them. On their return, it was time to divide the wealth and those who had gone to war wanted to deny those who had stayed at home from partaking of the wealth. This is what David had to say about it in verses 22 -25: "Then all the wicked and worthless men of those who went with David answered and said, "Because they did not go with us, we will not give them any of the spoil that we have recovered, except for every man's wife and children, that they may lead them away and depart." But David said, "My brethren, you shall not do so with what the Lord has given us, who has preserved and delivered into our hands the troop that came against us. For who will heed you in this matter? But as his part is who goes down to battle, so shall his part be who stays by the supplies; they shall share alike. So it was, from that day forward; he made it a statute and an ordinance for Israel to this day.

I mention this story to point out that everyone who is behind the scenes will partake of the same heavenly blessing on the day of reckoning.

When we first started at Bescot Market, our man of peace was the Market Manager Steve Evans, and his team. He did an excellent job in making sure that we got everything we needed each time we were in Bescot, and although he is retired, his sons, Scott and Spencer Evans, have followed in their dad's shoes to partner with us and it has been a fantastic partnership. They are simply brilliant at what they do. The Lord bless you, and reward your labour of love abundantly.

Now to the current Father's Heart team. Some have been with us from the start. We have become a family and are still open for likeminded labourers to join the vineyard of the Lord. They are Hyacinth Nelson and Nwanneka Nwokolo from two different churches, John Oliver, Bukky Iyol from my church, the Church at J10, and we have Juliet Chikore and Patricia Chang also from J10, who join us when they can.

I have mentioned these names because it is good to give honour where honour is due. They have laboured with me all these years, come rain, come shine and even in the snow. They are happy being there to share the good news of Jesus Christ. They are the ones whose feet are beautiful, as it says in Romans 10:15, "How beautiful are the feet of those who preach the gospel of peace, who bring glad tidings of good things," and in Daniel 12:3 it says, "Those who are wise shall shine like the brightness of the firmament, and those who turn many to righteousness like the stars forever and ever."

I truly thank God for every thought of each one of them. They have helped in furthering the Kingdom of God and in the thousands of seeds sown. My ultimate thanks go to the Almighty God who saw something different in me and considered me faithful to serve HIM. I echo the words of Paul in First Timothy 1:12, and it states, "And I thank Christ Jesus our Lord who has enabled me, because HE counted me faithful, putting me into ministry." May all glory be to HIM alone.

CHAPTER FIFTEEN

FOLLOWING JESUS

The life of a Christian is wonderful when we wholeheartedly follow Jesus Christ. HE did not say it was going to be easy, but HE did promise to always be there, every step of the way. Jesus came that we might have life and have it more abundantly (John10:10). Life without Christ is empty. People can have all the money, fame and all the acquisition of this world but without Christ, their lives are empty. They are not living life; they merely existed. Life is found in Christ alone, the author of salvation. God is the all-sufficient one who created all things and knows all things. Psalm 36:7-9 says this, "How excellent is thy loving kindness, O God! Therefore, the children of men put their trust under the shadow of thy wings. They shall be abundantly satisfied with the fatness of thy house; And thou shall make them drink of the river of thy pleasures. For with thee is the fountain of life: In thy light shall we see light."

Knowing God through Jesus Christ brings satisfaction. If we say we know HIM and walk in darkness, then we do not know HIM at all.

But when we live life through Christ, we see things differently and are content because we know that HE is faithful and will take care of the rest. Living life with Jesus at the centre brings fulfilment. In John 15:16, Jesus said,

"You did not choose me, but I chose you and appointed you to bear fruit and that your fruit should remain, that whatsoever you ask the Father in My name HE may give it to you."

Following Jesus does not bring suffering or poverty, it brings fruit, peace, joy, and an abundance of it. I do not mean just physical needs, but all-round provision, because HE is the one that gives us all that pertains to life and godliness. Jesus is the embodiment of the Godhead. If you have Christ, you have everything.

HIM choosing us means that we are HIS friends. In the same chapter of John, 15:14, Jesus said to HIS disciples, "You are My friends if you do whatever I command you. No longer do I call you servants, for a servant does not know what his master is doing; but I have called you friends, for all things that I heard from My Father I have made known to you." Being a friend of Jesus means you get to spend time with HIM and the more you do that, the more you become like HIM. When Moses was invited by God to the mountain and he spent forty days on the mountain with the Lord, his countenance changed, and the children of Israel could not behold his face when he came down because his face was glowing so much.

Spending time in God's presence means that we get to hear HIM clearly, we receive direction, divine strategies, guidance, and the blueprint of how, what, and when to do things. You only need to have the 'why' and you are good to go.

When Moses was on the mountain, having been invited by God, he received the Ten Commandments. Also, Jesus said to HIS disciples "Whatsoever I receive from the

Father, I have made known to you." In the same way, when we intentionally create space, and spend time studying the word of God, praying and praising God, HE downloads into us, and we too are equipped to do HIS bidding.

We do not want to be like the sons of Sceva, who thought they could cast out evil spirits in their own strength, but they learnt the hard way when the demon-possessed man overpowered them and beat them black and blue. Without Christ we can do nothing, but with HIM we can do all things. Surrendering to Jesus and spending time with HIM transforms and empowers us. There are protocols for everything in the Kingdom of God just like in the systems of this world. Surrender your life to Jesus, spend time studying your bible, pray with understanding and fellowship with other Christians in a bible-believing church and you too will do great things for the Kingdom of God.

I do not know what passion God has laid on your heart. It might even be a business venture or a ministry. Whatever it is, keep the light aglow. Do not let the vision die. You might begin to wonder how you are going to do it. The more you think about it, the more overwhelming it could become.

Remember that HE who called you is faithful, and HE will fulfil what HE has planted in you. I have shared my experience and how it all started. I had the 'why', but did not know the what, when and how but in the place of prayer, God opened the door and brought like-minded people to join me. I certainly could not have done it alone; following Christ should not be a lonely journey.

HE will bring the right people and the resources needed to fulfil that vision or calling. Having said that, we must position ourselves to be righteous before God.by trusting HIM all the way and obeying HIM as well. We should not lean on our own understanding, but in all our ways we should acknowledge HIM and HE will direct our path." (Proverbs 3:5).

HE has made provision already for all you need. Do not let your flesh get in the way and do not compare what God has asked you to do with what others are doing, especially if they are failing ministries or businesses. Psalm 118: 8 says that "It is better to trust in the LORD than to put confidence in man." Let us trust HIM. Remember when Jesus fed the five thousand with "five loaves and two fish," as recorded in the gospels, the multiplication did not start before they began to share the food. It started after Jesus took the five loaves and two fish from HIS disciples, gave thanks, and handed the food back to them. In obedience, they began to distribute the food, then the miracle took place. God is relying on our obedience to do what only HE can do. Let us not limit HIM by trying to analyse the logistics with our head knowledge. If we cooperate and partner with HIM, things should begin to fall into place, and we should see God move in that situation.

Twelve years on from our inception, we are still in Bescot Market reaching the least, the lost and the marginalised and still enjoying it. The battle is the Lord's, let HIM fight it.

There are times when we ask for things in prayer or have even planned for things to happen in a certain way and at a certain time. When those things do not happen as we expected, we become deflated and downcast. Be patient and wait for it and it shall surely come, just as it is recorded in

Habakkuk 2:3; and it says, "For the vision is yet for an appointed time; But at the end it will speak, and it will not lie. Though it tarries, wait for it; Because it shall surely come, it will not tarry." That's just like the farmer who sows seeds. He must first plant the seed, water it, wait for it to sprout, water it a bit more, weed, place mulch around it, tend it and when harvest time comes, the sickle will be out and ready to bring in the harvest.

I have to remind us that some seeds take longer than others to germinate, so waiting times may differ. As the farmer waters the seeds, we should water those God-given plans, businesses, visions and so on with prayer. Do not tuck the seed away in the soil of your heart and leave it there without watering it with prayer. Doing that will result in failure. We must trust God who gave us the plan/talent, knowing that HE is more than able to accomplish what HE had started.

I remember being burdened with some issues in my life. So, I prayed, fasted, praised, and I waited a bit more and I was now getting a bit impatient at this point, and the Lord spoke to my spirit and he gave me Hebrews 10:35-38. It says, "Therefore do not cast away your confidence, which has great reward. For you have need of endurance, so that after you have done the will of God, you may receive the promise: For yet a little while, and HE who is coming will come quickly and will not tarry. Now the just shall live by faith; But if anyone draws back, my soul has no pleasure in him." God knows the best time for you to launch that ministry or business. Trust HIM. Just like my team and I did. We spent a good six months praying and studying the scriptures and that is how we grew in confidence and got started.

Like the scripture above says, we need to do the will of God concerning the matter first, and be patient, then the fruit will come. Patience is a bit like faith. You do not see the result before you have to exercise patience. You must just trust and believe God.

Those things I prayed for a while ago, I am ticking the answers off my list, one by one. Patience teaches us reliance and dependency on our heavenly Father instead of depending on our own strength or ability.

Following Christ requires us to be teachable and humble. The fact that we are passionate about what God is calling us to do does not mean that we are knowledgeable in that ministry or in operating in that gift. We must be open, and willing to learn from others in order to grow. Joshua tagged along with Moses when Moses was the leader.

He even spent more time in the tent of meeting seeking God than Moses did. When it came to succeeding Moses, he was the perfect person to take the children of Israel to the promised land, because as he was serving Moses, he observed how things were done. Most importantly, how Moses sought and reverenced God, and he followed in those footsteps. He was there when God parted the Red Sea through Moses' rod and when he found himself in the same situation, as he led the Israelites to Jericho through the Jordan river, he knew what to do. In second Timothy 2:1-2, the scripture says, "You therefore, my son, be strong in the grace that is in Christ Jesus. And the things that thou hast heard of me among many witnesses, the same commit

thou to faithful men, who shall be able to teach others also."
We must humble ourselves and learn from seasoned and
experienced Christians so that we too can teach others who
look up to us. Following Christ requires us to be responsible
and accountable to our calling.

We must be ready to make some sacrifices in order to
drive the agenda and purpose of God in our lives. There have
been times in the team when we have had to sacrifice family
time, fellowship in Church with other Christians, especially
when there's a big event on. It might mean denying
ourselves certain things to meet other people's needs.

There were times when we met people who were really
in desperate need of food, and we have had to put resources
together to provide or buy them that thing they so need.
For instance, a member of the team saw the desire in one of
the traders to join our Bible study group. Still, her phone
was an antiquated one that couldn't download anything.

So, she took it upon herself to give her a good sum of
money to go towards a new phone. Today, that trader is one
of our regulars in the study group. There are many such
instances, but the point I am trying to make, is that as a
follower of Jesus Christ, you must be ready to make
sacrifices in your life, either with time or money, comfort or
belongings, and so on. This shows that we are putting God
first before all else. The joy is identifying with Christ
because HE said whoever follows HIM should first deny
himself or herself and come follow HIM. It means Christ
first, then everything else follows. It means looking out for
the needy amongst us and being sensitive to other people's
needs as we serve in humility. It means forbearance where

you would have been standing your ground, but at the same time, being bold as a lion when you need to be.

Let me encourage you even more. I had a dream at some time in this journey and I saw a big tree in front of me, and as I looked on, the branches were stretching out in all directions. There was an abundance of white fruits on the tree, and as I stood there, it was as if a hand shook the tree, and the white fruits were all over the ground. I began to pick them up but there were not enough of us for the number of fruits on the ground. God was showing me that the ready fruit will come and all I had to do was to pick it up without much effort. When we go out, we sow so many seeds, thousands we have sown over the years.

Some of them we have harvested, some seeds others will harvest at some point. For us then, let us concentrate on sowing seeds and harvesting the ripe ones which other people have sown.

There have been times when we've watered seeds and weeded the garden by offering people a shoulder to cry on, encouraging them, discipling them and doing life with some of them. No matter the stage, let us be thankful and stay focused on the "why." Building attracts conflict; so, by partnering with Jesus, we allow HIM to lead us by HIS precious Holy Spirit, knowing that whatever the challenge, HE will take care of it.

Endurance bears fruit. Jesus endured the cross to bring many sons and daughters to glory. Just like the Good Shepherd, HE will take care of every matter. Whatever God has given you, lay it down before him that you might pick it up again. When Moses laid down his staff before the

Lord and picked it up again when God instructed him, it became a defining moment in history because of the miracles he then performed with it. We too should learn to lay down before HIM what God has given us and I know that when we pick it up again, we too will have signs and wonders to testify about to the glory of God.

Bescot Market is a place of joy, laughter, friendship and pain, but HIS grace is more than sufficient. We will occupy and remain in office until Jesus returns. Shalom! Shalom!

Let Me Pray For You

You might be wondering what to do and how to begin your journey as a follower of Christ so that you too can enjoy life to the full. Well, I am delighted to help you. Jesus loves you and would love to welcome you into HIS family because HE has great plans for you. This is the single most important decision you will make in your entire life. The heart of our heavenly Father is love. The bible tells us that God so loved the world that HE gave Jesus to die for our sins. Sin is inherent in man because of the sins of Adam and Eve. In Second Corinthians 5:17 it says, "Therefore, if any man is in Christ, he is a new creation; old things have passed away; behold, all things have become new." For us to become part of God's family and enjoy HIS love and eternal life, we must be in Christ, and being in Christ means accepting HIM into our lives as our Lord and Saviour. In Acts 2:21 it says, "And it shall come to pass that whoever calls on the name of the Lord shall be saved." This is an open invitation for whoever will and an opportunity not to be missed. It is not about what we have or have not done but because of what Jesus did on the cross of Calvary for us when HE, being righteous, died for the sins HE did not commit.

There is a process to salvation and this is found in Romans 10:9 "That if you confess with your mouth the Lord Jesus and believe in your heart that God has raised HIM from the dead, you will be saved." All you have to do is to sincerely pray this prayer with me:

'Dear Father, I come in the name of Jesus Christ. According to your word in Acts 2:21 which says that "whosoever calls on the name of the Lord shall be saved" I ask you Jesus to come into my heart. I am sorry for all my sins. Father, I believe with my heart that you raised Jesus from the dead. I now confess the Lord Jesus as my Saviour. I am saved; I am born again, and I am a child of the Almighty God, just as it says in First John 3:1. Praise God!

If you prayed that prayer with all your heart, let me be the first to congratulate you and welcome you into the family of God. This is a lifelong journey, so join a bible-believing church near you and begin your Christian walk. Drop me a line or contact me via any of the ways that suit you, as listed below.

Email chiosuji2021@gmail.com

Facebook Chidi Flourish

LinkedIn Chidinma Osuji

TikTok Chidi Flourish (Chidiflo)

Website chiosuji2021.wixsite.com/flourishingmind

God bless you in your Christian walk.

ABOUT THE AUTHOR

Chidinma U. Osuji a devout Christian, with a unique passion for evangelism especially in the marketplace, still takes the gospel of Jesus Christ to the least, the lost and the marginalised.

She is also a retired Nurse, a Charis Bible college graduate, a mother and grandmother who loves to cook for her family and friends. Chidi the widow of late Dr Ezerulamaka Charles Osuji, has turned life around with God's help, and lives in the United Kingdom with her family.

ALSO BY THE AUTHOR

THE VICTORIOUS JOURNEY.

In this maiden effort, Chidi chronicles a hand-in-hand walk with a Guide unseen, but One whose presence pervades her most eventful life, from birth to adulthood. This is an intimate account of a journey through the life of an African girl, from innocence, through sorrow and courage, to a victory that could only have been by divine enablement!

*D*ear reader/writer,

I would like to take this opportunity to thank you for supporting one of our newest authors.

Here at Open Scroll Publications, we specialise in assisting talented writers to fulfil their dreams and aspirations. The creative process is hard enough as it is without having to worry about getting your masterpiece published once you're finally done. That's why Open Scroll Publications was formed. We demystify the process of getting published, and give a literary voice to those who would otherwise be muted in obscurity.

Our list of gifted writers is rapidly growing, and I would like to invite you to consider becoming our next distinguished author. So, whether you're working on a novel, a children's book, a poetry anthology, or an inspirational non-fiction piece, why not take a leap of faith and contact us? We would love to hear from you.

For more information, please visit us at:
www.openscroll.co.uk
info@openscroll.co.uk
Phone: 01213502422
       07506677504

Or write to us at:
Open Scroll Publications Ltd,
Kemp House,
160 City Road,
London, EC1V 2NX.